The
Imminent Rains

Line drawings by Hilary Heminway

The
Imminent Rains

*A Visit among the Last
Pioneers of Africa*

by

JOHN HYLAN HEMINWAY, JR.

LITTLE, BROWN AND COMPANY · BOSTON · TORONTO

Published simultaneously in Canada
by Little, Brown & Company (Canada) Limited

PRINTED IN THE UNITED STATES OF AMERICA

To My Father

Dear Manley,

I haven't seen a copy of this my first book for 25 years. It brings back strange memories and the faces of many good folks, white and black, whom I met on the way. Alas, there are but few of them left. I am lucky to be able to see many of our then dreams now actualities. How times change. Pioneering in those days was regarded as a rather decent sort of job — now most home folk seem to rank it one degree below burglary. But I notice they enjoy the proceeds. Anyhow it has been a great lark, hasn't it?

Yours,

Ewart S. Grogan

October 12, 1929

The . . . intruder into their solitude is always rewarded, and,
if he is sympathetic without showing it, is gladly welcomed in
spirit and with spirits . . .

—Gerard Wallop, *A Knot of Roots*

Acknowledgments

THIS book owes its existence to many people. Almost without exception those of whom I write welcomed me to their homes with solid hospitality. There are still others who, although they do not appear in the pages that follow, did as much, if not more. I hope that in a very small way this book will express my gratitude. In particular I wish to thank Mary Anne Richdale, my companion on this long safari, for her patience and enthusiasm; Quentin Keynes who first interested me in Africa, and who has since bombarded me with new adventures; Sally Wedgwood in Marandellas, Rhodesia, for her enormous hospitality; Peter Beard in Nairobi and New York for his advice and the use of his library of Africana, and Liam Lynn of Nairobi for a very gamey three weeks "out in the blue" of Kenya. I am deeply grateful to Edith Camp who gave me excellent critical advice; to Stanley Hart, my editor at Little, Brown, who believed in the book long before I did; to Fritz Fuerst, Patrick Thompson, and Doris Trace without whose help I might never have been able to leave Johannesburg; to Mr. and Mrs. Charles W. Engelhard for their hospitality in South Africa and for a delightful safari with them in the Masai-Mara, and to Mr. Harry Oppenheimer for many kindnesses, and his interest in this book when it was first conceived. Finally, I owe a great deal to my sister, Hilary, for her illustrations, her constant encouragement, and, above all, her patience.

The
Imminent Rains

CHAPTER I

"I am very old," he said gravely. He added, as a matter of course: "I'm glad to die in Africa."

"And why?"

"Because this is where mankind began. . . . One dies better at home."

— Romain Gary, *The Roots of Heaven*

As soon as Mary Anne and I entered the bar, the Welsh bartender set out to discover my motives for being in Mtwara, a remote town on the Tanzanian coast, and before I had finished my long-awaited drink he was already trying to discourage me from my plan. His moustache, in the shape of a buffalo horn, rose and fell on what must have been a well-muscled upper lip.

"You'll never be able to get down to Latham Leslie-Moore's house," he said. "And it doesn't make any difference whether you've got a Land Rover or not, because M'simbati Island is separated from the mainland by a creek, and don't you go telling me either that that Land Rover of yours floats. You could always try to get a dhow to take you across but, there again, these local chaps are not going to work on a Sunday. If you take my advice, drive north to Dar es Salaam and don't bother yourself with old cranks like Leslie-Moore, for you can be bloody sure that if you do visit him the only thing you'll get for your troubles is some buckshot up your tail end. The man is one hundred percent around-the-bend." The Welshman

In all parts of Africa you will, I believe, own the truth of the poet's words: 'noble found I ever the Native, and insipid the immigrant.'

— Isak Dinesen, Introduction to *Olive Schreiner,* Story of an African Farm

put a wet rag on the counter and with a circular move-
ment of his arm began to scrub off the dried beer stains.
"What's more," he continued, "you'd be well advised not
to ask questions around here. Just a few months ago a
journalist was taken out of bed in the middle of the night,
questioned and then shipped out."

And so it had gone. He might have surmised from the
beginning that I had resolved to visit Latham Leslie-
Moore and that nothing could shake me from my purpose.
I certainly would not have traveled an uncomfortable road
for nothing, suffocating with the dust and gasping against
the heavy coastal atmosphere which preceded the rains.
But the bartender evidently could not tolerate interest in a
rival character, and as a final attempt at discouragement,
tried to convince me that Leslie-Moore was irreparably in-
sane. "You know what the old fool does?" the bartender
said to me in a stage whisper. "He stands on the beach and
says to the sea, 'If I didn't have you I'd go mad.' And that's
not all: one time he tried to convince me that the only way
to plant coconut trees is to do it at night under a full moon
and to make sure the middle eye of the nut is facing
Mecca. Never heard bigger rubbish in all my life."

The next morning when I awoke I was not prepared for
the oppressive heat of the coast. Even before I arose, soon
after sunrise, the room was like a kiln and later, when I
stepped out onto the cement stoep of the room, my eyes
dazzled by the brightness, the sun stung my bare arms and
legs. The tide was out and the little flat town appeared to
be sitting on the edge of an enormous slag heap of exposed
coral. At breakfast in a room whose only decoration was a
bottle of Eno's Fruit Salts I pored over an admiralty chart
with Robert Stjernstegt, a young tsetse fly officer whom I

*In England I would be
one amongst millions
of people, here I am
king.*
— *Bob McConnell,
Fisheries Officer,
Lake Rudolph, Kenya*

had met briefly the previous night. We discovered that
M'simbati, Leslie-Moore's island, was separated from the
coast only during the rainy season when the creek filled
with water; otherwise it was connected to the mainland by
a dry riverbed. My Land Rover, therefore, appeared to be
the most reliable means of reaching the old man's house, although I was not confident that the last five miles of our proposed route along the beach to his house were negotiable.

At a reed village called Zwani, deserted but for two
women pounding mealies like the pistons of a rusted steam
engine, we left the coast road and picked up a faint track
which led us through copra and cashew plantations. Brittle slivers of coral broke through the sandy soil and cut
gashes into the tires. The river, as we had predicted, was
dry. We whined through it in four-wheel drive and soon
came to the village of Mtandi, where a man draped in a
bright-red *kikoi* introduced himself as a reliable guide.
"*Wapi bwana mzee kidevu*? Where is *bwana* old beard?"
we asked. The brightly dressed man assured us he knew
the way and with a crooked hand he pointed to a well-worn
footpath that wove between huts and cooking fires in the
direction of the beach. He climbed up on the hood of the
car and, as we slowly followed his index finger, he threw
triumphal stares at his fellow villagers.

Once we had reached the hard sand near the water I
released the four-wheel drive and flew along at a great
speed as though we were on a tarred road. Our guide sat
erect and stiff on the hood, not daring to turn lest the wind
catch his *kikoi* and blow it over his head. Evidence of his
soapless life blew through the ventilators until, suffocating, we shut them.

Beyond the lapping of the water, mangrove trees, like

headless waders, grew out of the sea, and, a mile distant, the receding tide exposed the shrimp-colored sand of Mana Hawanji Island. On our left coconut and cashew trees shaded the occasional dhow which had been pulled high up on the beach to escape the tide. Women with wet *kangas* clinging to their skins were returning to Mtandi carrying baskets of shimmering *dagaa*, a small fish like whitebait. Thousands of knot birds the size of butterflies were creating a flurry over the sea on their annual migration from Siberia. Our guide indicated with his hand that we had passed Ras Luvula Point and that we were now opposite the house of *bwana mzee kidevu*. We came to a stop. Through the trees whose shadows turned the thorny ground into a patchwork of light beams I saw what appeared to be an Arab fort. At first the only signs of life were some Africans who came down to peer into the windows of the car, but then, as if on cue, the huge teakwood doors of the house opened and an extraordinary looking man appeared. He wore a Panama hat and, around his waist, a *shuka*, a diminutive length of cloth. In one hand he carried a long walking stick, pointed at one end, and in the other, a gnu-tail flyswat. I was happy to note he was unarmed. His stomach was a massive, handsome affair — well rounded, nicely browned and very self-assured. When he was near at hand I noticed that his face bore a striking resemblance to that of King Edward VII.

"I want you to know," Latham Leslie-Moore said, "that the last time I had anything to do with anyone was at the Battle of Agincourt. However, for you I might make an exception." He looked at me out of the corner of his eye as though I, too, must not be taken seriously. "I've told the 'boy' to set extra places at luncheon."

We left the car by the sea and followed Leslie-Moore to his house. It was as I had thought, a fort, although not an authentic one. Around it were planted Indian cork trees, Casuarinas, oleanders, Nandi flame trees, frangipani and a cluster of purple bougainvillea. The shuttered windows and the thick lime and coral rock walls, crenelated at the top, made the inside of the house refreshingly cool. It was as though I had walked into an English country home. Leather-bound books covered the walls of both the library and the sitting room, and in a corner was a set of Waterford decanters containing sherry and brandy. On a side table there was a highly polished eighteen-pound shell standing next to a silver christening cup. Both rooms were lined with pictures of old friends — women with wasp waists in high-necked dresses and men in stiff white collars. The ceiling of the house was supported by mangrove poles and sleepers which had been appropriated from the Tanganyika Railway. Two swallows that nested in the "Tanganyika Railway" flew back and forth through the Arab doors. They constituted a danger only to those who were in a vertical path from their perch.

We stayed for the day and when, in the late afternoon, the heat became bearable we plunged into the sea and peered through goggles at the giant clams, helmet shells, augers and cowries on the bottom. Not far from the beach were huge clumps of coral and billowing marine ferns which sheltered lethargic groupers, parrot fish and, occasionally, an octopus. When we came to the surface we clung to the sides of the Mariamu, the old man's fishing boat which he kept anchored offshore. He stood on the beach with his dog Simba, pointing occasionally to where he believed there was an interesting coral formation. A year before he would have swum with us but now old age, he explained, had weakened his legs.

We left just before it was too dark to see and returned through the shadows to the town. The old man had invited Mary Anne and me to return on the following day, and although I was apprehensive that the rains might come and leave us stranded by the rising river, I felt that the island and the old man were more important than the threat of the rains.

Latham was waiting for us on the beach the next morning. He had put on a red-and-blue *shuka* and had instructed his staff of six servants to be equally well dressed. On the previous day I had told him that the bartender in Mtwara was jealous of his status and ever since then Latham had been building himself up to a fine Irish rage. "What can you expect?" he insisted, easing himself into his chair in the sitting room. "He comes from a Welsh coal pit where he worked in his youth and knows no better. After his aborted career in the army and several years on the bum he took over the pub when he had heard the previous owner had shot the moon. He's been robbing people ever since and no one has a good word to say for him. For years he has been trying to put people off from coming to stay with me. Stuffs them up with a lot of lies about me and the place, the object being, of course, to make them stay in his revolting pub and spend money in the bar. Don't pay any attention to him. We don't. Whenever he gives me any of his gaff I laugh like a closet. The poor man never knows what to do. Once, when he was his usual rude self, I turned to him and said, 'Stand at attention when you're speaking to an officer!' My God, he rose like an arrow."

Contrary to what I had expected, I gradually realized that Latham Leslie-Moore was not altogether a misanthrope. He lived a secluded life, but not to spite the world. On the contrary, people both white and black played a constant and important role in his world. A few hours of each day were devoted to correspondence with his friends and in the evening he regularly tuned in to the news on what he called his "talky box." Admittedly, thanks to the inaccessibility of his island, few people ever attempted the journey, but while he regretted not being able to see many of the old faces that once peopled his life he was delighted that he did not need to deal with the unfamiliar. Several months after my visit he wrote me a letter to explain how he felt:

To me, civilization ended in 1914. Since then it has been madness piled on madness. I fought in the wars and I know that the politicians of all countries are to blame: the lust for power and the money-grabbing by illiterate low-born crooks everywhere including the States, England, etc. They have given power to these savages in Africa long before they were ready for it and look at the mess the continent is in now. [In Tanzania] England sold out to them in '61, not caring a damn what happened to us. All they wanted was to get out quick and not spend any money. Thus started the "winds of change" which gave these blacks their independence. Now we are reaping the whirlwind. . . .

I live here alone on my island and I don't have anything to do with anybody. I am disgusted with civilization, with crooked politicians, police, prelates and, most of all, the press: the four p's that should be exterminated en masse. *Then burn all flying machines, radios, propaganda machines; eliminate all Pop, Jazz, teen-agers, Beatles, etc. and come back to what it was in pre-1914. Then you may regain your sanity. At the moment I have no hope for the world. End of message.*

Latham's pre-1914 world is not just one of maudlin
memories and nostalgia. The gallant retreat from the familiar to the exotic which he has practiced many times
dates back as far as his youth. There was once a time when
he felt himself synchronized with the world, but gradually,
when the element to which he was accustomed began to
crumble, he escaped into the timeless places. Smallfields
House, outside of London, a huge rambling country estate,
was where he began. He remembers the hunts, the fabulous pewter collection, the night his father won a bet by
jumping his favorite horse over the dining-room table
without disturbing the crystalware, his first sight of an automobile in the days when the vehicle was required by law
to be preceded by a runner with a red flag, and the time, at
the age of five, when he escorted two very old ladies to a
bawdyhouse in Paris. He and his brother studied at Hei-
delberg University, but their education there was brought
to a sudden end by the Irish Revolution which led to the
repatriation of their father's real estate. All the family income, which had come from rents in Ireland, was cut off,
and overnight Latham was left penniless. Rather than sulk
over his ill fortune, Latham decided to test his luck in
other parts of the world. He sailed to Trinidad and then to
Mexico, where he worked as an oil-rigger for several years.
His vacations were spent in Hollywood, where he acted
under the stage name of Larry Larsen in the company of
Mary Pickford and Douglas Fairbanks. When he returned
to England he was hardly wealthier than when he had left
it, yet he speaks of those days with heroic splendor. Once,
when I suggested in a letter that he cut a good figure in his
shuka on M'simbati Island, he replied: "Yes, I know I am
the best dressed man in Africa. I was that in England

. . . where I was considered the most elegant man-about-town. I was the introducer of the colored evening-dress tails with knee breeches and buckled pumps, silk stockings, white tie and a white waistcoat, of course. Of these I had two: one royal blue and the other plum-colored. Terribly smart we were in those days!"

And when in 1914 that fatal shot rang out in Sarajevo precipitating Europe into a "war to end all wars," Latham calmly followed the dictates of his class by joining the army as an officer. Under the command of General Gough he battled his way through France, until toward the end of the war he succumbed to mustard gas at Amiens. Doubled over like a hunchback, he returned to England to nurse his damaged lungs. A few days after his return he was informed by a doctor that he had only six months to live. Upon hearing the news he sat down in his club and, over a drink, explained his predicament to a friend. The latter suggested that he go to Canada for a spell in the outdoors. "The air is fresh and clean there," his friend said, "and I'm sure that after a few months your doctor will recant his verdict."

"Splendid idea," replied Latham. "I'll sail on the first ship."

Six months in Canada made Latham a new man. He returned to England fitter than he had ever been and decided after a few days that he had had enough of staying at home. The coffee market was booming and since he knew one or two things about agriculture he decided to put his hand to it. He set out for East Africa and when he docked in Mombasa made his way to Arusha in the north of Tanganyika, which Britain had recently claimed from Germany as a result of the Treaty of Versailles. His first stop was the local club, where he ran into an old friend. Over a drink the latter said, "We've put the locals to planting coffee and we're desperate for assistance. Need instructors and all that. Think you might give it a go?" Without a second thought Latham replied, "Delighted to lend a hand for the next few weeks, old chap." And so began a career which was to last for twenty years.

From the very first day as an agricultural officer Latham gained a reputation as a hard taskmaster. "It was a wonderful life," he remembers. "Everybody was friendly and there was no nonsense with the natives. If one got out of hand all you had to do was go up to an *askari* and say, 'Give him twenty,' and that solved the problem." He was particularly uncompromising with the Indian community. At the beginning of each day Latham inspected the Indian truck drivers who transported fruit upcountry from the coast. While they stood at attention he examined each one, and those who were unshaven or wearing soiled clothes were given correctional treatment on the spot.

As an agricultural officer Latham was always on the move. For almost thirty years he was never in one place long enough to call it home. During a two-year period at Mikindani he spent only eight nights in his house; the rest of the time he was in the bush. These few days of permanency were looked forward to with longing, for privacy was hard to achieve while on safari. On one occasion when he was in town an Indian entered his house and offered to line his pockets if he were willing to overlook an infringement of the law. No sooner had the suggestion been made than the bewildered man was forcibly thrown off the balcony into a thorn tree in the garden. "The Indian community never forgave me for that one. The chap should have known better than to disturb my siesta."

If your Honour will so far rejoice my soul to this extent . . . I shall pray forever as in duty bound for your Honour's life-long prosperity, ever lasting happiness, promotion of most startling rapidity and withal the fatherhood of many Godlike children to gambal playfully about your Honour's paternal knees to heart's content. . . . I pray your most excellent superiority to grant me this benign favour for Jesus Christ's sake, a gentleman whom your Honour very much resembles.
— letter from Gokal Chand, a Station Master, to his employer, from J. A.

While on safari Latham's chief means of transportation was the bicycle. Africa, he found, was ideally suited to this vehicle since, thanks to an abundant supply of labor, a native could always be found to propel it with a forked stick along the flat and uphill stretches of road. Latham has consistently refused to travel in "flying machines." What is more, he has never bothered to learn to drive an automobile since "the noise is unbearable and the smell absolutely appalling."

Once when Latham was camped in a desolate part of the country the territory's Governor, who was on safari, happened by. The latter's aide-de-camp intended their safari to stay a good distance from the agricultural officer's camp because, as he told the Governor, Leslie-Moore was an eccentric of the first order. "Doesn't even wear European clothes," the A.D.C. explained. After the Governor had politely listened to this explanation he withdrew from the safari, saying that he had to relieve himself. When an hour had passed and the Governor had not returned, the A.D.C. grew anxious and set out to look for him. Finally, after a fitful search, he discovered that the Governor had gone directly to the camp of Leslie-Moore, with whom he was now in animated conversation. It turned out that Leslie-Moore and the Governor were old friends from school.

Latham has returned to England only twice since he left after World War I. On a coffee table in the sitting room are two leather-bound photograph albums, as reminders of those visits. "That handsome-looking chap in the plus fours," he said, pointing to one picture, "is me." There were photographs of skiing trips in Austria, weekends with friends at their country estates, and of sailing trips in Scotland. It was evident from the pictures that he had

Modern machinery and modern efficiency have got in their deadly work and romance is fast departing from the land.

— *Frederick S. Colburn,*
The Unbelievable
Game Country,
1927

never been without a pet animal. On his first visit to England he brought a lion with him. He used to walk along Piccadilly with it tied to a chain. One day he decided to lunch at the Ritz, a hotel of which he was not particularly fond. He arrived in the company of the lion and asked a terrified headwaiter for a table for two. As soon as they had been brought to their table the lion jumped into one of the seats on command. Latham turned to the waiter and said, "The steak for me and a plate of bones for my friend."

Latham first saw the island of M'simbati in 1933, and he vowed that when its owner Peshana Naranji died he would buy it and build a house on it. In those days the island was completely overgrown, the only signs of human life being the ruins of a hut in which a German had lived during the First World War and the eighteen-pound shells which the British had fired at him from offshore. In 1942 Peshana Naranji died and three years later the land was put up for auction. Latham discovered that his chief opponent in the bidding was the Aga Khan community, which had far larger financial resources than he. But by advancing the auction-house clock twenty minutes Latham contrived for the bidding to begin ahead of schedule and he bought the island before the Aga Khan's representative had arrived. Latham paid a little over two dollars an acre.

Latham is proud to observe that he has served under six monarchs, from Queen Victoria to Elizabeth II. He believes that as a civil servant he played a part in the maintenance of the British Empire and regrets that he was forced to witness its dissolution. When Britain granted independence to Tanganyika, Latham felt personally affronted. Overnight, it seemed, England had liquidated its responsibility to a loyal subject, and a new, foreign government was now his overlord. Latham decided not to allow such an apparent injustice to pass unnoticed. His solution was characteristic: he would form his own government. One night, after weeks of careful planning, the island of M'simbati seceded from the mainland. The island's constitution was established by a formal ceremony in which Latham and his houseboys took an oath, on a Persian rosary and a silver Arab dagger, to uphold the laws of the Prophet Muhammad, the Koran and Queen Elizabeth. "I have the honor to inform Your Excellency," he wrote Sir Richard Turnbull, then governor, "that on the last stroke of midnight, December 31st, 1959, this island of 640 acres seceded from Tanganyika Territory by the unanimous vote of all the islanders . . . We shall, of course, continue to help dhows and fishermen in distress, as heretofore, who have been wrecked on the reefs." Another letter was dispatched to Dag Hammarskjöld, Secretary-General of the United Nations, applying for membership on behalf of the ten inhabitants of the island.

For a brief moment Latham's little struggle for independence gained the attention of the press, and letters from all parts of the world poured in praising him for his defiant action. The East African *Standard* was moved to write in an editorial of December 17, 1960, "Today the English do not want to boast, or be reminded too often about their rough island story, but the path of duty is still the way to glory and especially when the path is trodden alone . . ." To those who wrote to him inquiring, Latham explained that his object was to "remain under our Queen and stay loyal to our country, thereby keeping a tiny white island in a sea of black barbarism, to carry on the civilization of hundreds of years of culture that has been the heritage of our race." For almost two years the M'simbati flag flew over the island. In its upper lefthand corner was the Union Jack, to symbolize the island's loyalty to the Queen; the rest of it was covered by three bold stripes: one emerald-green, one sea-blue, the other bloodred. Let the emerald-green island of M'simbati, the flag signified, forever be separated by the blue sea from the bloody shores of Tanganyika.

It was Latham's finest hour. In one of the press releases he warned, "Let no man think he can take advantage of a survivor of General Sir Hubert Gough's immortal Fifth Army, that fought the battles of the Somme, Messines, Ypres, Polecappelle, the Menin Road, Passchendale and the epic retreat of March 1918 where, outnumbered four to one by the Germans and outgunned six to one, we fought them to a standstill in eight days: the greatest fighting retreat in military history and the turning point of the war. I learned to fight for freedom there under the inspired leadership of our famous general and, by Allah, I will fight again if necessary. The spirit of the Fifth Army lives on."

Latham's typewriter began to clatter regularly every morning, issuing threats to various officials for having insulted the island's sovereignty. Just before Christmas, during the island's secession, he was visited by an American journalist. Latham, wearing but a *shuka*, waded out to his boat and demanded both his passport and landing card. Saying that he would present the passport to the magistrate Latham took it ashore, leaving the journalist stunned. A few minutes later Latham returned and reported that since the visitor did not possess a landing card the magistrate had ordered him to be confined to the island for a period of three days in order to keep Latham company over Christmas.

During the secession Latham would wake up at his usual hour of 5 A.M. and ask himself, "Whom shall I be rude to today?" Once he had chosen a victim he would write him an insulting letter containing as many uncomplimentary epithets as he could think of, generally ending it with a "P.S. Rude letter follows." Once, without his initiation, a provocative situation arose by itself. The pilot of a small plane dropped Latham a note weighted down with a ham sandwich on the first Friday in Ramadan, a very holy day for Moslems. Latham, uncharacteristically polite, drafted the following letter to Sir Frederick Crawford:

It is with regret that I have to inform Your Excellency of the following incidents, both of which occurred here yesterday, Sunday, March 6th, 1960.

While the majority of the islanders were at prayer in the Mosque, a flying machine, coming from Mtwara, flew in very low, at treetop height, over the houses and the Mosque, causing great consternation as some of the islanders have never seen a flying machine before . . . This is a violation of the Island's Airspace Regulations.

This flying machine then went towards the South and returned in a few minutes. When it was over the Mosque and the houses, while still at a very low altitude, a port hole was opened from which a hand protruded and threw out a packet which landed in the shamba. *It contained pig products . . .*

I do not know if it is the intention of Your Excellency's Government in Tanganyika to precipitate a Holy War on the continent of Africa but I cannot conceive a method more likely to do so than to pelt members of Islam while at their devotions with pig products from the air . . .

I have refrained from bringing this to the notice of the Sheikhs of Islam in Zanzibar, Mombasa and Dar es Salaam until I have a reply from your Excellency.

An investigation lasting several months was made by the government into the matter and when it was discovered that, in fact, the incident had not been intentional it was finally dropped. But by now the government of Tanzania was becoming more embarrassed than anything else by Mr. Leslie-Moore, so finally, in November 1961, a gun boat was dispatched to the island to quell its secession. Latham directed a few choice oaths at the officer who had presented him with the government's orders and then marched him off the island with a gun in his back. Latham refused to lower the flag until sunset. At six that evening all his houseboys were drawn up in formation outside the house and they watched as the M'simbati flag was lowered for the last time. "It was a sad evening," Latham told me. "The end of the greatest laugh."

On the night before Tanganyika's independence, Sir Frederick Crawford paused before he returned home to England to say farewell to Latham Leslie-Moore. Although the two had never met, they had become friends. "I cannot leave Tanganyika," the Governor wrote him that night, "without thinking my farewells to the country's most southerly outpost. I send you my best wishes for Christmas and the New Year and for a long, happy and undisturbed continuance of your sojourn on M'simbati Island. I am sending you a little fluid sustenance [a bottle of Scotch] as a parting gift. We shall think of you . . ."

Although M'simbati's secession is over, Latham's life remains as it was. Every day he tends the chickens, administers the gardening and fills the giant auger shells with water for the birds in front of the house. He makes a small income from the cashews and the coconuts, but the market for copra has been weak and this year it failed altogether,

leaving him with twelve thousand coconuts in his store-
room. Every night, before retiring, he reads. He used to
subscribe to *The Illustrated London News*, but when it introduced colored covers he dropped it. At the beginning of
every month he waits for his copy of *Blackwood's Magazine*, which he considers the only worthwhile periodical
left. In a recent letter he told me that he has started to
swim again. One of his servants, Mariamu, stands by in
the shallows to help him onto his legs. Sometimes he takes
the island children into the deep water and teaches them to
swim. His only concession to intemperance is a sweet ver-
mouth; which he may allow himself when he has visitors.
On special occasions he sends one of his "boys" up a tree
for a *madafu*, a young, sweet coconut, and adding a touch
of gin to the milk, will drink it out of its shell. He insists
that it loses its flavor if it is poured into a glass.

M'simbati is where Latham has come to rest. He has
retreated as far as the sea and now there is no place further
to go. For him, there is a great sense of belonging. He is as
important a feature of the island as the red-eyed weavers
flitting through the frangipani, — the dogs walking along
the beach with him in the late afternoon, his "boys" whom
he has known for so many years, and what he calls the
"Rose du Barry pink" of the sunset. He has not left the
island for two years, not even to go into Mtwara, and he
does not intend to ever leave it again. At his death his
"boys" have been given strict orders to roll up his body in
the M'simbati flag and to bury him in a clump of coral
behind the house.

In the middle of my last night on the island I was awakened prematurely by the cockcrow. I looked through the
shutters and noticed that the sky was bright with stars. I

got out of bed and walked along the corridors of the fort to the outside. Simba the dog began to bark and soon Latham came out to investigate. Standing barefoot on some rose thorns we listened to the whispering of the wind in the palms. Latham pointed out in the distance the mutton-chop sail of a *jihazi* slipping into its last anchorage in Tanzania before making its passage south along the Mozambique coast. Orion was bright in the night sky and far away the Southern Cross was about to fade. "Lovely night," Latham said. I nodded. "Bloody worthwhile," he continued, "being an eccentric, don't you think?"

POSTSCRIPT: One year after our visit to Latham Leslie-Moore he was removed by the government from his island. The Mozambique border, thirty miles from M'simbati, has become a scene of fighting and all the country in its vicinity has been declared restricted. As I write this (September 1967) he is in Mtwara waiting to find a place to live, not knowing what has become of his servants. The East African newspapers suggest that he was subjected to cruelties while being taken into Mtwara and that his island is being used as a base for the training of African freedom fighters. His last letter is addressed from Wind's Whisper, but in it he explained that this was to be the last letter from the island. "All my life savings," he wrote, "have gone into making a lovely place of Wind's Whisper. Now my house will be looted and will fall down. The birds will have to go elsewhere for their drinking water as I cannot expect anyone to fill up the drinking shells on the forecourt walls, and eventually, over all my land, the bush will reclaim its own. This is the end of everything for me . . .

"Perhaps when things have settled down in Africa, in a few years' time, you may come back to M'simbati to see the old place and rest on the beach and remember the days that have gone."

CHAPTER II

"I feel like a thief," I whispered to Flint. "I'm taking something away from this country I never brought into it — romance."

"Well, help yourself freely," he whispered back. "We'll never miss it."

— Daniel W. Streeter, *Denatured Africa*

My INTENTION was to drive into the interior of Bechuanaland and to have a look at what are called the Sand Plateau and the Okavango Basin. The map seemed to apologize for Bechuanaland, as though it would take responsibility only for the words "desert" and "swamp." On most geographical matters, it was ambiguous. Lakes were marked with dotted lines, tracks with the warning "dry weather only" and parts of the desert with an illustration of an unexplained plant. The words "spillway," "pan" and "vlei" were used in the absence of more concrete names. Everybody at Kasane told us that in Bechuanaland maps were useless. Far better than a map, they said, was a man who knew the country.

Robert Bacchus, a young Englishman and a professional hunter, offered to join us. He had over a week of spare time before his clients were due to arrive. "Not worth spending all that time in the bar at Kasane," he explained when he accepted our invitation. I told him that I intended to drive as far south as Maun, two hundred miles from Kasane, and then travel north by canoe into the swamps. He knew the road to Maun but he had never explored the swamps. A crocodile hunter in Maun who, he assured us, knew them as well as any man, would give us all the assistance we needed. Once we arrived in Maun, Robert would speak to him about arranging a safari by boat.

Early one morning, a few weeks before the rains were due, we set off for Maun. I had let air out of the tires as a precaution against the deep sand, discarded all our nonessential supplies, except for a case of Southwest African beer, and filled the tank and jerricans with fuel. I could see it was going to be a hot day. Even in the early morning pulsating waves of heat rose from the track and distorted the horizon. The game had dispersed from the water holes at an early hour and the footprints of elephants which just minutes before had been full of water were now drying and becoming hard like rocks.

As soon as we had left the game reserve the road deteriorated. It had never been graded and the surface was uneven and rough. We pitched and rolled from side to side, always on the brink of going too fast or getting bogged down in the sand. We raced through villages spreading the dust high into the air. Kavimba, a group of huts overlooking the Caprivi Strip, and Kachikau, consisting of an abandoned trading store and hundreds of potbellied children, were the last settlements we were to see for many miles.

After five hours of driving we turned off the road to a camp, near the Selinda River, which Robert's firm maintained. Our intention was to spend the night there and the following day try to reach Maun. The road was constructed in a casual sort of way. It snaked around trees, through bushes and over the stumps of mopani which pro-

truded a few inches from the light soil and were as rough
and brittle as coral. As we rounded a sharp corner, my
eyes lifted from the road in time to see a male kudu. His
corkscrew horns were enormous and during the brief moment that we stared at each other, both mesmerized by a
seemingly foreign presence, I noticed that his body was
quivering as though he was preparing himself to fly off in
any direction. He stood still for only a second. Suddenly he
was off, leaping across the road and, as though separated
from the ground, sailing into the deep bush.

After twenty-two miles we came to a wide clearing
shaded by an enormous fig tree. Nearby were several forest-
green tents and a group of Africans who had been left to
maintain the camp in the absence of the hunters. A hundred yards from the camp was the Selinda Spillway, a vast
sea of papyrus stalks stretching to the west, each one arching delicately over a background of transparent water.
Cutting through these thick stems was a narrow canal just
wide enough for the small outboard kept by the hunting
firm for spotting sitatunga, the elusive antelope of the
swamps.

In the afternoon when a cool wind began to blow, drying the sweat on our faces, we set off into the swamps for a
brief look. I stood in the bow of the boat and poled through
the narrow channel until we reached the river. Robert
started the engine, and soon we were sweeping along in the
current toward the south. We trolled through country
which was devoid of trees and landmarks. On a few high
stretches of ground the vegetation had been burned. The
sitatunga, which often grazed upon the rich green grass
that grew amidst the charred remains of the papyrus, were
perfect targets for the hunters' guns, although, as Robert

said, because of the high waters this year, few had been
shot. We passed the carcass of a hippo on a bank. It was
crisscrossed with spearmarks and its stomach was distended and gurgling.

Once we had lost the smell of the rotting carcass, the
green jungle of reeds spreading for miles on either side of
us brought to us a feeling of tranquillity. Although it was
only green it seemed to be forever changing in texture,
shades and shape. The breeze would occasionally reach us
when the weeds on either side of us thinned, bringing with
it the smell of decaying vegetation and of wood smoke
from our camp. Dusk soon crept over us. It came with a
feverish abruptness as the sun lost itself in a haze far
above the horizon. Briefly it poised like a crystal of lemon-
yellow in the green distance which was neither sky nor horizon. And then suddenly the haze reduced it to a pallid
glow. In the heavy stillness of evening, shadows crept
through the green of the bush and along the lines of our
faces.

The next morning we left camp and retraced our tracks,
now covered by the spoor of buffalo, lechwe and wilde-
beest. When we reached the main track we turned south
and within a short time we were driving on the Mababe
Depression, a huge expanse of baked earth bordered by
water holes.

Not until the 1870's was the Mababe first seen by white
men. On their treks from South Africa through Ngamiland to the rich elephant grounds of the Chobe this was
often the only water hunters saw for many miles. In 1876
Martinus Swartz, a Dutch elephant hunter, and ten members of his family died of fever in Mababe. Two years later
Frederick Selous reached here when his cattle and horses

were on the point of collapsing from thirst. In *A Hunter's*
Wanderings in Africa, published in 1890, he wrote of this
experience:

Just before sundown, we emerged upon the great open plain
known as the Mababe Flat, and old Jacob at once pointed out
to me the smoke of some grass fires which were burning at a
distance of about twelve miles. "Those fires are burning in the
reeds of the Mababe river," said the old man. I looked at my
poor, hollow-sided, jaded cattle, and then again at the distant
smoke, and wondered whether they would all be good for the
journey. We now saw a great many zebras about the flat, and
I said to old Jacob that I felt sure that there must be water
nearer than the river, or otherwise how could the presence of
so many zebras and the buffalo spoor be accounted for. The
old fellow said there were some pans just within the edge of
the mopani, close to us, but as the large vleys we had passed
were dry, he did not think it likely these little ones would still
hold water. However, we went to look, and five minutes later
found a long shallow vley full of water. I could have hugged
the dirty old man with delight. What a sight it was to see the
poor thirsty oxen come trotting down to the pan, as soon as
they smelt the longed-for water, and rush knee-deep into it!
What a sudden relief the sight of that pool of muddy water
was, too, and what a weight of fear and anxiety it lifted from
our hearts! Only an hour before it had seemed that I was
doomed to lose all my live stock — nearly everything I possessed in the world — from thirst; and now the danger was
past and not a single ox had given in.

Selous stayed in the Mababe for several weeks in order
to rehabilitate his cattle. On his first day he shot two lion-
esses, and on his second, three lions and two giraffes. But
the country was thick with tsetse flies which, together with
the heat, made life unbearable, and he was only too glad to

leave. For thirty-one years no other white man was known to have visited the Mababe. In 1909 after a rinderpest epidemic which destroyed most of the game, Arnold Hodson, a sub-inspector of the Bechuanaland Protectorate Police, retraced Selous's steps. Unlike Selous (and Livingstone before Selous) he noted that the Mababe was free of tsetse flies. What is more, he found it was inhabited by Africans. They were "very low class," he reported, and did not "have much feeling of any sort." He illustrated his point by explaining that the natives discovered lion kills by watching the flight of vultures in the early morning. As soon as they had pinpointed the spot they would locate the remains of the animal, scare off the hyenas, jackals and carrion birds and eat what was left. Hodson notes in *Trekking the Great Thirst: Travel and Sport in the Kalahari Desert*, "The mangled remains of an animal killed by a lion and covered with grit, saliva and blood would not offer a very attractive meal I should think, but *chacun à son gout*."

When we drove through the Mababe there was little game to be seen. The sun was high and whatever animals lived in this desiccated country had sought the shade and were grazing on the edges. The buffalo alluded to by Selous have by now been almost completely eliminated, but since Hodson's time tsetse flies have returned and are just as great a nuisance as they were when Selous tramped the country. While the Zwezwe Sands, an infamous eight miles, reduced our progress to a crawl and almost doubled

our fuel consumption, for Selous it was an agonizing ordeal. The wheels of his wagons would become buried in the sand and the oxen, thanks to the crack of his whip, were forced to strain to a point just short of collapse. Every inch was won by brute force.

By noon we had covered the worst part of the track. Gradually the desert changed to bush. Mopani trees, like scattered corpses, sprung up on either side, interspersed with brittle slivers of grass. Occasionally we saw sable antelope with horns like Chinese swords and herds of giraffe, their long necks whiplashing backwards and forwards with each gallop. In spite of the seemingly sparse vegetation and the lack of water the game seemed sleek and round.

At Tsotsoroga Pan, one of the landmarks on the map, a huge ground hornbill was drinking near the track. At our approach it refused to fly until we were almost upon it. Running, it looked like a turkey, and once it finally stretched its wings it became a nanny in a huge overcoat scurrying over the ground in pursuit of her charges.

The mopani were interspersed with acacia trees, which were taller but, like the mopani, gave little shade. At Jovorega Pan Robert found a drum of petrol which he had left buried in the sand a year before. We siphoned four gallons. Even on the edge of this little water hole the country was bleak. Every tree, every bush seemed to be a replica of a former one. Nothing moved except the flies, which swarmed about us on waves of heat. One could easily get lost in this country. Miles and miles of the same landscape could make a man lose hope: never a hill or a river to break the spell of aloneness. I remembered the story a trader once told me of how when he was trekking this

For a long time, while the sun rose and the day became hot we drove through what Pop described, when I asked him what the country was like to the south, as a million miles of bloody Africa, bush close to the road that was impenetrable, solid, scrubby-looking undergrowth.

— Ernest Hemingway,
  The Green Hills
    of Africa

country in the thirties he stopped under a tree to rest and found a gun and the skeleton of a man and his dog lying nearby against the same log. When the trader reported the incident to the District Commissioner in Maun he learned that this man had been in a hunting party a year before. One evening he set out to shoot guinea fowl and never returned. For three days his companions searched for him. Finally they lost hope and, convincing themselves that he had been killed by a lion, they resumed their journey.

Thirty miles from Jovorega Pan we came to a Bushman village called Kudumane. The people were not of pure Bushman stock but were of a hybrid race called Masarwa. The difference was slight: apart from being slightly taller than the Kalahari Bushmen they had the same high Mongoloid cheekbones, Oriental eyes and tightly knotted "peppercorn" hair. Near Kudumane in 1878 Selous found some Bushmen. He described them in *A Hunter's Wanderings in Africa* as

a family of three-quarters starved Bushmen. It is a marvel how these poor wretches managed to keep body and soul together. They had been living for a long time past on nothing but a few small berries and an odd tortoise, and were in such a fearful state of emaciation that it made one shudder to look at them. Their hollow shrunken faces looked like skulls with dried skins stretched tightly over them. All the flesh on their limbs seems to have atrophied, the knee and elbow joints and the bones of the pelvis standing out in unsightly knobs, whilst (owing to their having to eat a great quantity of very unnutritious food to sustain life at all) their stomachs were enormously distended; altogether they were as pitiful-looking objects as it is possible to imagine.

Soon afterwards we passed along the border of the

Moremi Wildlife Reserve. It contains vast numbers of red lechwe, giraffe and eland and is one of the few game reserves in Africa in which sitatunga antelope exist. What is more, the Moremi Wildlife Reserve is the first tribal game reserve ever created in Africa. In March 1963 this area of seven hundred square miles was set aside by the Batawana tribe, the owners of Ngamiland, as a game reserve. Since the area consists of shallow swamp it is virtually useless to them as a grazing area. They believed that by making it into a game reserve they could generate a source of funds to support it and it would provide them with a steady flow of revenue; but they soon discovered that because of the Moremi's remoteness, tourists have been scarce. Only with the help of the World Wildlife Fund has the Moremi been able to survive. As a result, the aim of game conservation is far more direct and genuine in the Moremi than in other parks: here the protection of animals exists solely for itself and not for the benefit of tourists.

Beyond the Moremi, huts and small villages begin to appear on the side of the road. A few miles before Maun we stopped at a tsetse fly control post in the middle of a wide clearing. It was a corrugated-iron shed similar in design to a tobacco-curing barn. One end of it was opened to allow us entry. Once we had driven inside the doors were shut behind us and we were enveloped in total darkness except for a square of light filtering through a frosted-glass window. The purpose of this building was to prevent tsetse flies from being carried by automobiles from a contaminated area into a fly-free area. These flies have spread over most of the wooded parts of Bechuanaland, particularly in the northeast. They are about the same size and shape as a common housefly, except for a long, narrow, striped abdomen. Unlike the housefly, which absorbs moisture and salt off the skins of animals by means of a retractable sucker, the tsetse has a set of syringes which penetrate the skin to draw off the blood of its prey. Contained within the salivary enzyme they secrete through these syringes to prevent the victim's blood from clotting are sometimes trypanosomes, the parasite that can cause sleeping sickness. A very small percentage of flies carry the trypanosomes, but the threat of contracting sleeping sickness convinced us to use a fly spray in the car whenever we passed through a contaminated area.

The tsetse fly is only a carrier of the trypanosomes. It acquires them from noncarnivorous animals who are immune to the parasites and may carry large reservoirs of them. The only creatures who succumb to trypanosomiasis are domestic animals and man. Cattle and sheep will not last very long if they are allowed to graze in fly-infested areas. *Nagana*, as trypanosomiasis is called when it strikes animals, will reduce a healthy animal within a period of weeks or months to skin and bones. Unless it is treated it will die, but the vaccine is expensive and beyond the means of most ranchers.

There are three ways in which tsetse flies can be eliminated. One is by clearing a belt of bush two hundred yards wide. Research has shown that the fly's eyesight is one vulnerable aspect of its constitution. Since it is unable to see over two hundred yards it will not attempt a flight of that distance unless there is something in the foreground on which it can alight. Therefore, the range of the tsetse can be checked by an organized system of bush clearance. Another way to eliminate the menace is by spraying the bush with insecticide. This method requires airplanes, expensive machinery and a tremendous amount of man-power. In general, it has proven to be uneconomic in Africa, where thousands upon thousands of square miles would have to be treated. The last and certainly most controversial method is game clearance. By shooting such hosts of the trypanosomes as duiker, lechwe and warthog the flies would no longer be a menace. But since these animals are small and elusive this method is impractical.

The success of tsetse eradication depends upon the use to which the land is ultimately put. Unless it is settled immediately after being cleared of tsetse, it will revert to its original state. The tsetse fly control therefore has to make certain that once a piece of land has been made fly-free it will be grazed by cattle. In Bechuanaland, however, most of the land contaminated by this insect is useless for cattle since it contains little water and few roads. Settling new land today would be very expensive, far more than it was for the early settlers who could choose fly-free, well-watered country and were not dependent upon roads. What is left of the wilds, particularly in Bechuanaland, is, as Selous said, "wretched, waterless country."

Someday research will discover how to immunize men and animals against trypanosomiasis, and prospectors will find hidden wealth in this barren country and water will flow freely. Then this land will contain hope for people who would otherwise starve because of overpopulation. But it is a proven fact that ever since man began to settle virgin land in Africa the game have suffered. There was a time when the game could well afford to suffer, but today almost every species is on the thin wire between survival and extinction. When the game is gone much of the high hopes and expansiveness of men will also disappear, and

Africa will not be as big or as interesting for future generations as it has been for us. But neither men, nor governments, nor virgin land, for that matter, can escape the future. This track connecting the interior of Bechuanaland with the outside world will someday be free of sleeping sickness and *nagana*; it might well become a major thoroughfare connecting communal ranching complexes, and with them will come telephone lines, steel windmills and herds and herds of thin cattle. And so the sunsets will be bleached by the dust of passing cars, the eland and giraffe will be talked about only as myths and the "old track" first attempted by Selous with a salted horse, a herd of cattle and several pairs of tough boots will have lost its past and gained in its place merely the distinction of being a thick red line on the road maps.

The doors of the tsetse fly control closed behind us and two officials wearing epaulettes and badges marched up. Saluting, they rapped their heels together and goose-stepped the length of the building. At each step they counted to ten while spraying the car with DDT from archaic bug bombs. The flies swarmed out, flew to the ray of light at the window, and soon fell to the poison. The ceremony lasted ten minutes, and once it was finished the atmosphere inside the shed was stifling. After we had reviewed the two control officers in one final display of their military training, we drove the last few miles into Maun.

Maun looked like a railway siding. The most permanent objects in the town were forty-four-gallon petrol drums which cluttered up the front of the trading stores. The buildings were made of strips of corrugated iron and looked as though they had been intended to last for only a few weeks. The town had made little impression on the desert: the buildings were far apart and separated by sand, and the roads were only tracks going from one trading store to the next or from someone's house to the bar. At best Maun seemed to be a place where travelers stopped to collect their wits and organize their provisions for another safari.

The center of town was the bar at Riley's Hotel, a white cement structure filled with dusty trophies and ale-polished teak. When we arrived in Maun just after sunset the bar was full. At one end hovered a polyglot group of racial hybrids. There were Bushmen, Hottentots and Hereros and combinations of each, sometimes mixed with European blood. They spoke in either Bushman dialects, Tswano or English. At the other end of the bar were the European contract men. There was, for instance, the local police force, consisting of Paddy, a ruddy-faced Irishman dressed in white shorts, and his assistant, a young Englishman who had just completed his two-year tour of duty. Nearby was a group of traders standing about "Smelly" George Kiriakou, an old Cypriot with a face as angular and lined as a woodcut. His son told me late that night at the bar that his father's trading stores operated on the basis that minimum profit on a transaction was thirty-three percent, one hundred fifty percent was the median. Their five stores, some of which are accessible only by dugout canoes, average one thousand pounds profit a month. Skins have become one of Botswana's most important exports, he told me. Twenty years ago a leopard skin would fetch five pounds at the very most; today they sell as high as fifty. A coat, he claimed, made of five skins and sold in Europe or America would cost thirty-five hundred pounds. "It won't be long," he assured me, "before we get our share of the profits which stores in America are making. Just give us time."

Next to "Smelly" George Kiriakou at the bar was George Ross, Kiriakou's accountant. He was wearing a wide R.A.F. tie and a ragged white sports coat. He was drinking alone. I introduced myself and talked with him briefly. Never taking his eyes off the bottles at the back of the bar he told me that for him Maun was just one stop among many. I looked down at his hands and noticed that he was missing a finger. Several hours later I asked someone how he had lost his finger. "Oh, yes," I was told, "that was bitten off by his wife two weeks ago. His wife, you see, is the local chief's daughter and cost two hundred pounds and didn't feel that her charms should be squandered on Ross."

At this end of the bar was also the doctor, an enormous man with very thick eyeglasses who recently had abandoned England because he did not believe in socialized medicine. He explained to me that although his duties as doctor were far beyond the capacity of any human being, he liked the job. There were fifty thousand square miles of country which fell under his sole authority. The national airline, which he used every week to make his tour, allowed him only a few hours in each of his dispensaries. Most of his cases were sleeping sickness and malaria, both of which can only be cured by a long convalescence. "I lose many battles out here," he explained, "because I don't have either trained men or beds or medicine." A little while later I was asked by someone else, "What did you think of the doctor?" I answered equivocally. "Poor chap," I was told. "Just the other night his wife ran off with a white hunter, and his daughter with the son of the D.C. It seems he's so nearsighted he didn't see what was going on until it was right on top of him."

New faces kept coming into the bar. Almost everybody was dressed either in shorts or in khaki drill and bore some sign of having recently lived in the bush: ten-day growths, full-length beards, unkempt moustaches and sunburns. There were white hunters, crocodile hunters and charter pilots — all taking a break from some mission. It was Saturday night and as good a reason as any to have a few drinks before returning to their lonely jobs, and everybody was in the spirit for buying rounds. Someone commented that it was not a very profitable venture because every time you bought a round there were at least ten recipients, and you could be sure of receiving only three or four drinks in return. When Simon Holmes-a-Court aged twenty-four, the game warden, walked in, everybody raised his glass to him and said, "have a drink." One old man confided to me that if he had a son he would be like Simon — "level-headed, resourceful and tough." Later on the head of a safari firm walked in and the old man turned to me and said, "Now, there's a man for you. You won't find anybody more honest. Wouldn't mind having him for a son either."

As the night progressed the humor became obscure and the beer became warmer. I overheard a burly hunter talking about his friend "old Daryl," whom he called the "maribou stork." "Why a maribou stork?" someone asked. "Well, old Daryl has legs like a stork and he eats everything. You know, one time I found him eating a scorpion."

Elbows leaned on the teakwood bar and the thin layer of beer which lay over everything crept up shirts and jackets. One hunter poured beer down the front of his shirt to cool his stomach. Beer lay on the floor like thick glue and made

When a pilot in the Desert Locust Control wired headquarters

FOUND LOCUSTS COPULATING

he was promptly answered:

STOP COPULATING

the air heavy and stale. One conversation soon led into the all-encompassing subject of dining in the bush. Someone complained: "I've been eating canned corned-beef hash for the past three months and I'll tell you one thing: from the way it tastes it couldn't be corned-beef hash — more like mealie meal mixed with trek oxen."

Someone else suggested, "I reckon when you add Mrs. Ball's chutney to it, it isn't so bad."

"Look man," said the first speaker, "let's leave Mrs. Ball out of this."

Outside it was crisp with the dryness of the desert. We drove for a few miles to a piece of cleared ground on the bank of the Thamalakane River. After we unloaded the car I lay on my camp bed with the wind nudging at my unbuttoned shirt and I listened to the river rushing by. In the bar Robert and I had spoken to Billy Cornuel, a crocodile hunter, about the Okavango Swamps. There was only one way to see them, he explained, and that was by boat. There were no roads, no proper airstrips, no Europeans and very few Africans. Just water, grass and crocodiles, he sighed. If I wanted to be outfitted with a boat and a guide, it could easily be arranged. Bobby Wilmot, his boss, was away, but he had the authority in Wilmot's absence to let me go. I mulled over the plans as I lay on my camp bed and, when I had fallen asleep, dreamed about all the water we were going to see.

It was Sunday. The bush did not recognize holidays but Maun did: the town, except for the bar, closed down and anybody who could have been of some help to us had disappeared into the bush. We lay in the tall grass and spent the day reading back issues of magazines. Late in the afternoon we packed the car and drove to Bobby Wilmot's camp. Billy Cornuel and Lloyd Wilmot were there and we had dinner with them around a brazier made out of half a forty-four-gallon petrol drum. The "old man," Wilmot, was expected back from Francistown any time now. I was told no one could possibly keep a check on his movements; one moment he was here on the Bouro River, the next he was on the Nata, and the next he was in Shakawe. The natives call him *Nyangasa*, which means "hurry here, hurry there." "You will see when you meet him," Cornuel had said.

The mosquitoes came with the night. We fought them with helpless swats and curses and moved closer to the fire to get away from the sting of the night air. We used glowing sticks of wood to light our cigarettes, and when we reached too close to the fire the hair on the backs of our hands would curl and burn. Billy and Lloyd did most of the talking. The conversation was like plainsong, sung by one and answered by another. The only interruptions came when someone asked for "disinfectant" (ketchup) or when laughter or silence cut off a voice. Then the night noises would creep in upon us.

Lloyd looked far younger than he actually was. It seemed as though life in the bush had let him live without pressures and compulsions. Throughout the night, while sanding a model airplane, he played records on a battery-operated gramophone. Sonny and Cher alternated with Viennese waltzes. He rarely lifted his head, even when he spoke, unless it was to examine the effect of some comment he made at the expense of Billy.

Billy was twice his age but the two of them seemed well suited to each other. Billy's supreme talent was dramatizing life. His world was filled with heroes and villains, with struggles between himself and nature, and with a long and baffling list of his adventures. He tried hard to do justice to his subjects, but often, it seemed, the presence of attentive listeners made him overenlarge the color, the details and sometimes even the action of his story. Often in the midst of his narrative the object of his tale would become lost to him, and then he would spend long minutes relating incidents which had not been very significant. Sometimes, when he felt we might not have appreciated the full import of his words, he would accompany them with a long shrill whistle and would shake his head violently. His South African accent, full of the earth and the barroom, suited him perfectly. His heritage had been in the bush and he was proud to continue it.

"Ah," he once said, "I've been everywhere a canoe can get to in the swamps. There is no place I don't know and yet, I tell you, the only places I like are the ones I haven't been to before. I'm bored going back somewhere for the second time. Tell me to go to a place in the swamps I've never seen and I'll be off like a flash. Yet, there is one place that I don't mind returning to now and then, and that's Jo'burg. As soon as the 'old man' returns to keep an eye on this place I'm going down there. Three months out here without a woman is all I can take. Right now I've got to cause some trouble."

Billy loved a good practical joke. His victims were generally innocent people who somehow stumbled into the swamps with him. Several years before, for example, he took out a party of hunters in search of a sitatunga antelope. One of them brought along his wife, a plain-looking woman who retired punctually at eight each evening. One day Billy caught a live baby crocodile. He taped elastoplast around its snout and then put the animal into the woman's sleeping bag. That night she dismissed herself from the company of the men at her usual early hour and once she was undressed, slipped into her bed. It took her only seconds to realize that she was not alone. "Damn it if she wasn't bare as a babe when she ran out of her tent — screaming as though the world had just come to an end."

Later Billy told us that the waters in the swamps were unusually high for this time of the year. As a result, lions had moved out of the interior and were within thirty miles of Maun — the closest they've been since anybody can remember. "I'll tell you," Billy said, "I've got a great respect for lions. I'll never forget what happened to me once. You see, I'd been hunting this lion for four hours. Man, was he a mean bugger, and after my first shot hit him in the shoulder he burrowed into the tall grass and waited for me to get too close. I knew where he was and I stalked to within twenty yards. I couldn't see him but my eyes were fixed on the spot where I knew he was lying. Suddenly he broke and came toward me like a thunder flash. I pumped three bullets into him and he still kept coming. I was desperate for I only had one bullet left in my gun. My last shot I fired as he sprang. The bugger died in the air and fell beside me. Up till then I had been sweating from head to toe, but when he died I lost all fear. I tell you, man, that bugger could have still been alive and ripped me all the way through. I just didn't care what I did — my mind had gone blank and cool like a snake charmer's and I walked up to him and dragged him back to camp. And then, damn it: twenty minutes later when I was sitting on a camp chair I started sweating and shaking like a madman. I thought I'd never be able to stop my teeth from rattling. I was as scared, man, as anyone's ever been. All this time that I've been living in the bush I've never been able to stop those shakes when I come close to getting the axe."

As the night wore on we crept up to the fire. Above us was a brilliant sky: the moon, almost full, illuminated every detail of the surroundings — the reed huts, neat and symmetrical, looked as though some child had cut them out of silver paper. All through the night a steady grinding noise came from them: termites, I was told. Thorn trees spread witches' fingers across a cobalt-blue sky, and on the branches of one of them a pair of tame guinea fowl murmured a sleep song. In front of us was the river bank and tethered alongside it, like oxen who had come to drink, were two native canoes. There was a gentle whispering sound about this place: the water lapping at the bank and the wind breathing through the high branches of the trees.

In Africa nights stretch for interminable minutes. For every rustle in the grass something new happens in the sky and yet the lights of the stars never change. For us, stopping in the midst of sentences to listen to a new sound, the night made us forget the future and the past. We were merely observers at a ceremony more solemn than we have ever witnessed before. The waters, it seemed, were too great to dam, space too wide to harness and civilization the only spoiler.

Very late at night we heard the distant sound of an engine. It grew louder and louder and soon we saw a truck racing down the narrow track to come to a halt in front of the camp, spilling the dust high into the night sky. It was Wilmot. He and his daughter Joyce had left Francistown at four that afternoon and had driven straight along the new road (sand, like all roads in Botswana, but graded).

I was expecting someone quite different. Wilmot seemed to be too small and slight to be a crocodile hunter. With a pair of plastic-rimmed eyeglasses perched on a seemingly fragile nose, he looked more like an accountant than a man who had lived all his life in the bush. What is more, unlike most people in Bechuanaland he had made no compromise with "African time." Life at high speed and with insurmountable difficulties was what he wanted. As soon as he arrived he rushed out of the cab of the truck and began a rapid-fire conversation with his son and Cornuel about his activities during the past week and what he expected should have been done in his absence. Briefly introducing himself to us, he unloaded the truck and shot words out to his son in an electric voice.

Wilmot was born at the end of World War I in a trading store his father owned in southern Bechuanaland. The country was so remote that not until 1925 did he see his first automobile. In those days, he admits, the game was far scarcer than it is today. Before he was born, an epidemic of rinderpest had killed off almost all the wild animals. Since then the game has gradually been on the increase and only in the past few years has it been checked by the trade in skins and the encroachment of native cattle. Wilmot believes the country has changed very little since the early days. Roads and airfields have been built in his time but so far they have done little to make Bechuanaland part of the rest of the world.

For the past eleven years Wilmot has been shooting crocodiles. He began when the crocodile skin market was just developing, and since then he has shot altogether thirty thousand of the animals. He is allowed two thousand annually by the government, but for a fee he can exceed that amount. Since the croc population in the Okavango Swamps has been diminishing rapidly over the past few years, Wilmot has been trying to convince the government to limit the hunting of crocs to ten months a year in order to allow the animals time to breed.

Wilmot has found that the best time to hunt crocs is at night. He stations one man in the bow of the boat holding a lamp while another one in the stern paddles. As soon as the glowing eyes of a croc are spotted the boat is paddled in its direction. Since the croc becomes transfixed by the light the boat can often approach to within inches before it panics. The paddler, who doubles as hunter, has ample time to raise his gun and take careful aim at a spot between the eyes. The first shot rarely kills a crocodile. The animal's hard crusty temple sometimes requires as many as five shots. Once the animal is dead it must be skinned, and the skin which is heavy must then be brought onto the boat. Once Wilmot had twelve skins on board his boat. He was so overladen that with only half an inch of gunwale showing he had to bail the entire two hundred miles back to camp.

The record crocodile for the swamps, measuring twenty and a half feet, was shot by one of Wilmot's hunters. Wilmot himself killed twenty-four of the animals in one day — a record he does not like to boast about. He admits that within three or four years crocodile hunting in the Okavango will be finished. Even today his hunters concentrate on the northern regions of the swamps since the crocs in the south have been virtually eliminated. Wilmot feels, however, that he alone is not responsible. Africans have learned from his hunters how to kill the animals on a profitable scale. With primitive muzzle-loaders and Martini-Henrys, some of which can be dated back to the time of Livingstone, they have reduced the crocodile population considerably. The one hopeful note is that only half of the swamps can be hunted commercially. There are a great many areas, Wilmot asserts, which are either inaccessible to his boats or are thought by the Africans to be inhabited by giant hippos and crocodiles possessed by demons. Wilmot once investigated one of these places and discovered a fourteen-foot crocodile which had learned to capsize canoes. Perhaps, and this was a "perhaps" which Wilmot was delighted to throw in my direction — perhaps the inaccessible half of the swamps contain the breeding grounds for crocodiles. If so, there is still a chance for them.

By now, it was very late. The fire in the brazier was a mass of glowing coals and the sky had lost its newness. I said good night and retreated to my camp bed behind one of the huts.

I awoke early in the morning to find the camp inundated with chickens. At breakfast they scrambled onto our plates of corn flakes and left little prints on the edges. Before us, lying motionless against the dock, was our boat. It was sixteen feet in length, of aluminum construction, and covered with a canvas canopy as a protection against the sun. We carried two twenty-five-gallon drums of petrol, and two eighteen-horsepower engines, one on the transom and a spare lying on the floorboards. In addition we brought on board enough canned food to last us for three days, sleeping bags, mosquito nets, a pressure lamp, and our treasured case of Southwest African beer. Our guide was called Xabutsi. He was a small man and undoubtedly of Bushman extract. His hair was tightly knotted, his skin was light and his face was formed into quadrants by deep lines.

We left Wilmot's camp early in the morning. I sat in the bow seat which was normally occupied by the lampboy. Directly behind me was Robert, and on his right sat Mary Anne. Our supplies, spare fuel and engine lay between us and Xabutsi, who had assumed a seat on the gunwale which he seldom left for the rest of the day.

We followed the Thamalakane River for three miles. It was wide and free-flowing and on either side we could see signs of life — some grass burning, a group of naked children watching us advance upstream, or a hut clinging to the skirts of the swamps. Two miles later we turned through a narrow opening which led through long stalks into the grass-choked Bouro River. The water was a mass of submerged vegetation. Every few minutes Xabutsi raised the propeller of the engine to clean it of weeds. The farther we went into the swamps the slower was our progress.

At the beginning of the Bouro we passed several dams made of acacia branches stuck into the river bottom to stop the flow of weeds downstream. Clogged with grass they served little purpose other than to add yet another obstacle to the river. Over an hour after we left Wilmot's camp we came to a small village on the west bank of the river. Xabutsi explained with his hands that it was a tsetse fly control post and that we would have to stop. When our boat coasted in through the weeds we discovered that it was abandoned. All the inhabitants were burning grass somewhere. On the ground was lying a Johannesburg mail catalogue showing fashions in men's and women's uniforms. It was dated 1946.

We were soon under way again. The river had become

wider by now and sometimes it was difficult determining where the bank ended and the water began. Water and sedge grass, wild rice and muxa (a thick green growth on which the sitatunga feed) enveloped us. Occasionally the reeds were so thick that we would have to stop the engine completely and advance by pulling on their long stems. The water was so clear that no matter how deep it was the slightest detail on the sandy bottom was visible. A strange red, knotted weed grew in the sand and gave the water, when seen at an angle, a warm pearly color. Once when my eyes were focused on the bottom I saw a young crocodile flash underneath the boat.

At first the trees were not very spectacular. They were of the hard, clumsy variety which always appear to be awaiting rain. Color was washed out of them, as though they were suffering from drought. The camel thorn (*Acacia nigrensis* or *Acacia giraffae*) and the acacia (*Acacia alpidar*) stretched olive-gray thorns into the sky. The only green tree was the *citamuzi*, but its leaves were so far apart that it gave little shade. It is called the rain tree by the natives because, during the months of September and October when the weather, as a prelude to the rains, is hot and humid, water pours from it. Recently the cause of this phenomenon was discovered. A small insect called a froghopper nourishes itself on the sap and ejects the spent fluid in a steady stream. Since the downpour can last for as long as two hours the effect is one of rain.

At midday we began to see palm trees. There was the *makoba* or vegetable ivory palm, a towering tree on which a nut the size of a pool ball grows. Xabutsi nibbled on one in the belief that it would restore his virility. There was also the phoenix palm, not as tall as the *makoba*, at the top of which the leaves fan out in a symmetrical sphere. The natives cut incisions in the bark of these trees and "bleed" them of their sap. Once this liquid is fermented it becomes palm wine, a highly intoxicating and thoroughly delicious drink. Trees which are tapped for the wine are never allowed to heal. Each time the incision appears to be closing the natives recut it until finally the tree dies.

We crossed the Garacau Flats — an endless sweep of water and reeds which was almost completely devoid of high ground and trees. According to Wilmot, when he first began hunting the Garacau was one of the richest areas in the swamps for crocodiles. Today there was no sign of life. It was easy to imagine Wilmot in this sort of country, a tiny figure lost in the maze of reeds and canals, peering through field glasses to find the telltale ripples on the water or eyes in the high grass. Sometimes, he told me, he would be gone for three months at a time. When he left his main camp on such a trip the boat was invariably overladen with forty-four-gallon petrol drums and food supplies. Once, in fact, it sank just a few miles from camp and he spent a whole morning retrieving the cans of food. When everything had been rescued he discovered that the labels had peeled off. "For two months," he said, "it was potluck at mealtime. I'd take out three cans hoping one was a soup, one a veg, the other fruit. More often than not I'd be stuck with three soups for dinner or three cans of fruit. Man, after a couple of months we acquired very tolerant constitutions." When he was traveling downstream he would often drop his extra drums of petrol overboard and let them float ahead while he hunted. Sooner or later the drums would be stopped by a blockage.

Wilmot was often lost for as much as two weeks. Each

island, channel or clump of weeds, as we discovered, looked very much like another. "But it didn't really matter," he said, "since we generally had enough food to see us through. Anyway, the sun and the stars were always there to give us directions, and sooner or later we'd find our way back to camp."

In the swamps the birds seemed to add an entirely new dimension to nature. Every reed quivered with a passenger, and the sky, which by itself was a forgotten blue, was brought to life by their flights. The most common bird was the white-throated cormorant, which, when sitting on the water, was almost completely submerged. As the boat bore down on it, it would stretch its wings, hesitate momentarily, as though the decision to fly required some thought, and then, flapping flamboyantly with the water glistening on its back like silver-plating, race to a spot farther upstream.

The Skwaka heron followed us into the swamps. It was a dirty brown-and-black bird which flew into the deep reeds as soon as we approached. The pied kingfisher was different for it would rarely fly when we approached. Camouflaged among the reeds, it was not interested in this child's game of hide-and-seek.

The Hottentot teal and the Pygmy goose also seemed to be heading for the center of the swamps. Beautifully colored, as though some artist had painstakingly dipped each of its feathers into a lustrous enamel, the teal flew out of reach of our cameras almost within seconds. The comic of the swamps is the African jacana or lily-trotter, a thin little bird with legs and webbed feet far out of proportion to its size. It walked as on tiptoe from one lily pad to the next, and when we approached too close it flew away with its legs outstretched behind it like stalks of asparagus.

Sometimes we would hear a sound above us like a feverish wind wrenching the leaves from the high branches of a tree, and then, looking up, I would find thousands of birds no larger than hummingbirds darkening the sky. They are called Quelea and they can devour a field of wheat within minutes.

We did not stop all that day, but continued on our slow path into the swamps until it became dark. After the Garacau Flats we again found ourselves in a maze of islands, floating sudd and a skeleton-like tangle of trees. Occasionally a fish eagle sitting on a high feces-covered branch would shatter the stillness of the late afternoon with its cry.

Going up that river was like traveling back to the earliest beginnings of the world, when vegetation rioted on the earth and the big trees were kings. An empty stream, a great silence, an impenetrable forest. The air was warm, thick, heavy, sluggish. There was no joy in the brilliance of sunshine. The long stretches of waterway ran on, deserted, into the gloom of over-shadowed distances . . . And this stillness did not in the least resemble a peace.

So wrote Joseph Conrad half a century ago (in *Heart of Darkness*) about another place. He could have been writing about the Okavango. The great emptiness of blue and green, of little fingers of vegetation and of tall arms of deflowered trees held the same silent sinister aspect. It was too abstract a place: the blur of basic organisms, the extravagance of water and greenery. A thousand things past, tainted with a heavy bleakness, labored through our minds. It was not the heat that discolored the vividness, but rather the pressure of being in the midst of such va-

cantness. This great elemental tangle of sedge and water-ways and pools and silence was frighteningly familiar. We all recognized it although none of us had been here before.

We had originally intended to camp on an island called Nyaraga, but since our progress had been better than ex-pected we decided to continue farther. Late in the after-noon we surprised a herd of elephants bathing in the river. With the sound of a waterfall they rushed out of the water, and then melted into the bush without a sound. Only a cloud of dust remained.

We turned into the reeds at an island called Mumu and, as soon as we reached land, began a fire. The hard ground was littered with the spoor of buffalo, lechwe, tsessebe, ele-phant, giraffe and impala. The sun soon disappeared be-hind a row of palms and the whole sky, transparent for a second, suddenly grew deep red as though a curtain was lifting on a gaudy stage. It paused for a second and then, with the distant bush seemingly scarred and burned, the red prismatically changed into black and the night sky swept over us with the flurry of departing wings.

After dinner we retired to mosquito netting. I looked up at the rising moon which throbbed with light and noticed its reflection on the branches of an African ebony tree and the leaves of a huge fig tree which swept over our camp. I could hear the grunting and yawning of a hippo and far away the lugubrious howling of a pack of jackals.

In the morning I was awakened just before dawn to the sound of the boubou shrike. The male whistled two notes and the female responded with a guttural garbling. Just after the first light an emerald-spotted wood dove began his whimsical ballad. The natives believe that he is saying, "My father's dead, my mother's dead and all my relations are dead. Oo, doo, doo, doo . . ." Accompanying him was the coucal, a small grayish bird whose sound is that of a pencil when it is stuck into the path of a fan blade. It is supposed to announce rain, but this time the coucal was in error as the rains would not come for at least three weeks.

We continued on our path into the swamps until lunchtime, when we reached an island called Txakwe, one hundred and five miles from Wilmot's camp. This was the furthest point we were ever to reach within the swamps. A month before, Billy Cornuel had led a party of anthropologists to an island fifty miles beyond here, where they made contact with the last survivors of the River Bushmen, a tribe consisting mainly of old men, some almost toothless, with the faded features of their desert heirs. At one time these River Bushmen had spread over all the swamps and as far west as Lake Ngami. Today they numbered only thirteen. All their days were spent moving from one island to the next in search of food. Their primitive methods of hunting had reduced them to an almost continual state of hunger. What is more, as one of the old men said, their luck was not as it used to be.

At Txakwe there were two empty drums of petrol and the head of a huge crocodile which Cornuel had shot as meat for the Bushmen. The jaw was propped open with a stick and rows of polished teeth disappeared into the shadows of the mouth. I wanted Robert to stick his head inside for a photograph but he said the smell was intolerable. Hanging above us, as though it had been buried Indian-like in the air, was an acacia in the arms of a fig tree.

It is a pity we did not continue deeper into the swamps. It seemed that we had fallen into the spirit of the country. Within its endless monotony I had learned to pick up details, to look at one blade of grass and not be overcome by all the rest. The paths of flattened reeds, the sounds of breaking twigs and a change in pitch of the stillness had all become of prime interest to me. But, we had a schedule to keep and reluctant as we were we turned back.

Just before the light began to fail we stopped at an island to look for game. The spoor on the ground indicated that elephant had recently come here to drink, and that the tsessebe, a faun-colored antelope, had grazed the island during the night. Clearly marked in the mud nearby were the pug marks of a large lion which had swum across the river. Through the long grass on the far side of a clearing we saw a female kudu and her young stretching their necks to catch more of our scent. Beyond them seven giraffes turned their heads and then ran in slow motion toward the farthest trees. It was clear that the game had reason to be uneasy about human beings. The entire Okavango Swamps have been hunted for countless years by the Batawana. But with primitive weapons they have made only a very small dent in the game populations.

The next morning, after having camped at Nyaraga, we continued our trip to Wilmot's camp. We were making good progress until suddenly, at 12:30, the motor coughed and stopped. I thought at first that Xabutsi might have shut the power off to clear weeds from the propeller. Soon, however, I realized that something else was the matter. His face, which was normally stern, became even sterner. He mumbled something in Tswana and from the tone of his voice I knew that he was saying we were out of gas. It was difficult to believe. Weren't the two twenty-five-gallon drums filled when we left? I discovered that only one had been filled to capacity; the other must have contained only ten gallons. Foolishly, I had not supervised the mechanical preparations for the trip.

There were no oars in the boat (even if there had been she was too wide to row) and between us and Wilmot's camp lay thirty miles of water. Our only hope was to wait for someone to rescue us. Since Wilmot expected us in the evening he would certainly come looking for us when we did not appear. But perhaps he might give us a day or two before he made the petrol-consuming journey and by then our food would be exhausted.

As a last resort, Robert and I unscrewed the floorboards and, stationing ourselves on either side of the boat, began to paddle back to camp. The work was laborious, particularly when the wind, which blew against us, turned the boat broadside to our course. Each stroke advanced us by mere inches. After an hour we estimated that we had covered only one mile. "Great rowing material we have here," I yelled to Xabutsi, who nodded his head because it was easier than saying he did not understand. "Next year," I continued, "we ought to represent Bechuanaland at Henley. Those boys at Eton would be hard-pressed to match our equipment. Let's see now, Robert would be stroke, I number two, Mary Anne number three, and you holding the engine." Suddenly Xabutsi started mumbling something. Either he thought we were making fun of him or, more likely, he was tired of getting splinters in his hands. "He wants to set out on foot," Robert translated. "He says the water is not too deep and that there's a village twenty miles from here where he can borrow a canoe." We gave him a tin of meat, the .3006 gun and a round of ammunition. We bid him good luck and he jumped over the side of the boat and into the reeds. His route would take him over

. . . and there the two great steam monsters lay hooting and whistling to each other in the night, in the vain hope of attracting attention and assistance — man's twentieth-century addition to the pachyderms of Africa.

— Sir Michael Blundell,
So Rough a Wind

hard ground and through water up to his chest. By six o'clock that night he hoped to be in Wilmot's camp. We estimated that Wilmot would take two hours reaching us and so, given a two-hour delay, we would be rescued and underway by ten o'clock that night. We paddled for another hour and then poled the boat through some weeds to a small island covered with dead thorn trees.

After clearing a patch of ground for a campsite and cutting some firewood, we sat in the shade of the canopy of our boat and I read an old copy of *Punch*. There was a story in it about a man who was trying to forge insurance forms. From the viewpoint of our little African Queen the idea seemed remote and useless to me. I put the magazine down and picked up Conrad's *Heart Of Darkness*, which I had been carrying in my bedroll. Far more to the point, I thought, as I read one passage. "No fear can stand up to hunger," he wrote, "no patience can wear it out, disgust simply does not exist where hunger is; and as to superstition, belief and what you may call principles, they are less than chaff in a breeze. Don't you know the devilry of lingering starvation, its exasperating torment, its black thoughts, its sombre and brooding ferocity? Well, I do. It takes a man all his inborn strength to fight hunger properly. It's really easier to face bereavement, dishonour, and the perdition of one's soul — than this kind of prolonged hunger."

Not that we were worried about hunger. There was enough food, in a meager sort of way, to last us through dinner. Tomorrow, however, there would be nothing. We were not alarmed because we felt sure that Wilmot would come, if not tonight, certainly by tomorrow. But the bush, as we all knew, was unpredictable, and, when we looked around us, the stale, wet vegetation twisting and turning in a labyrinth of weeds and islands and sudd gave little hope. Wilmot might not come for several days: he might have driven off to Francistown and left the camp derelict, or Xabutsi might run into trouble. Conceivably, it could be days before help came. Could we last? Several years ago I had gone without food for two days in the Sahara. Robert told me that once he did not eat for five days in the Kalahari, and Mary Anne was as hardy a creature as any of us. If help did not arrive the following day we would resume our paddling and, with luck, reach Wilmot's camp in two days.

In the evening we began a fire and cooked the last of our food. We finished off our Southwest African beer and settled down to watching the fire and listening for the sound of an engine. The flames sent sparks out into the grass and the beer bottles grew sticky in our hands. I kept remembering the words Robert had used once when I asked him why he had left England. "Too many people," he had said in his abbreviated manner. "I guess," he went on, "I just like my solitude." And that is what we had that night; each of us was left with his thoughts. They weren't melodramatic — about death or starvation — because we all knew that we would somehow manage. Our rescue was in the hands of other people and only as a last resort would we be called upon to save ourselves. I thought of a million things which did not pertain to our condition — of St. Helena, of a pack trip in Wyoming and of a half-forgotten face. Suddenly when the flames shot higher and a charred log tumbled off into the ashes the present flashed back. Absurd, it seemed, and yet strangely comforting while being stranded in the

LONE TREE CAMP
ATHI RIVER
Christmas Day
1905

Dîner

Soupe à la queue de Rhinoceros
Pâté de Poisson à la Chaumière
Dinde d'Athi rotie à la Percival
Legumes Mpishi

Boeuf Pressé au Stores

Plum Pouding à l'Anglaise
Fromage John Wellington et Gideon

Sardines
Biscuits
Fruits
Ticks

(signed)

C. A. Ward

W. H. Townsend Storrs

A. Blayney Percival

Beatrice Waterford

swamps to finally discover that, in the end, we were all intruders.

By midnight there was still no sound of an engine. I lit a pressure lamp and, walking down to the boat, I tied it to the frame of the canopy as a signal light.

Just before dawn I awoke. The pressure lamp had gone out and our camp was once again just a clearing in the midst of thorns and spear grass. We were still marooned. We breakfasted on three biscuits and the last of our coffee, packed our equipment and sat on the deck in silence, listening to the wind.

Almost exactly at nine o'clock, Robert heard the sound of an engine. I strained but could not hear a thing. I listened again but still there was only wind. And then faintly, as though it might be only my imagination, I heard the whining of a propeller being revved in the air. It grew louder and louder and soon the bow of a boat jutted through the reeds a hundred yards away. It snaked through the tall grass, pushed along by the wind. Wilmot was sitting on the transom, holding onto the engine as though it might jump out of his hands. His eyes behind a smudged pair of glasses roved through the weeds on either side. As soon as he saw us, he let the current push him into the elephant grass. He was shaking his head. "I'm sorry, folks," he said. "I don't know how that Billy Cornuel could have let you go without enough petrol. When I see him, you can bet his ears are going to be boxed."

Once again we were among friends.

CHAPTER III

All my old love of pioneering was roused, a love inherited
from my father and my American forebears. Perhaps it is
easier to grow roots in virgin land; at any rate, I had never
felt so strong an urge to put down new roots as I did in
Africa. The century of the common man was jealously destroying the uncommon man in the old world. By that I do
not mean arrogantly to imply that I am an uncommon man,
but such talents as I have seemed to have more elbow
room in Kenya.

— Gerard Wallop, Earl of Portsmouth,
A Knot of Roots

SHE was an uncommon woman. When she stepped onto the stoep of her house I could see it in the way she walked. At one minute she seemed to be engulfed by the enormity of the plain which swept out in every direction and in the next she seemed to be mistress of a colossal realm. She stood for a second squinting her eyes and then strode over to where we were. We met halfway under a towering fig tree, the only shade for miles. I reminded her that we had met briefly several years before. "Of course I remember," she replied. She invited us in for drinks and then for lunch. "Oh, for God's sake, why didn't I think of it before: stay the night." And then turning to me with a pixyish smile she said, "The only thing I can promise you is strong drinks."

From the very first moment there was something improbable about Erica Critchley. On the one hand she was as rough and as confident in the wilds as the toughest man. She dressed in a bush jacket and khaki pants and walked with long bold strides. Yet, her bearing and her outlook seemed to be far too urbane for this secluded life. Her conceit was charming, her opinions coquettishly cynical and her humor witty and biting. Hers was a laugh which could have been heard over the violins at Claridge's or against the call of the croupier in a chandelier-encrusted gambling club. She might well have been a member of that handsome vintage of Englishwomen who had lived through two wars, several husbands and many lovers with an undamaged bearing. Life had taught her to disarm men with a look of insurmountable boredom and a flick of the nose to remind them of their inadequacy. She had once lived this role in its completeness, but both it and the contestants had come to bore her. Instead she had chosen the bush as an arena for her charm and chic.

As a girl she had been sent off to school in England after her father discovered that the tutor he had imported from England was doing nothing more than teaching her the poem "The Battle of Blenheim." She attended three schools in quick succession, being expelled from each one because of her profanity. She admits that even at the age of nine she had a remarkable talent for swearing. Finally, as a last resort, her father sent her to school in South Africa. She remained there for several years although she never advanced further than the first form. She once told her father that she was the foundation stone of the entire lower school. He liked the idea and felt that such a position showed that at least she had class.

Every time she boarded the train in Livingstone for South Africa she used to invite her old friend the steward, and anybody else who looked decent, into her compartment for what she called "an old-fashioned booze-up." As she explained, "One should never arrive sober at school. What is more, it was unforgivable while school was in session ever to be found without a bottle on tap." She generally buried her bottles around the grounds during gardening class. As a punishment for slight misdemeanors the girls were made to plant gum trees. For most of them this was indeed a punishment, but for Erica nothing could be more fun. She loved gardening and the outdoors and also the opportunity to tap her whiskey supplies. "In fact," she added, "most of the trees at that school were planted by me."

Her father, F. J. "Mopani" Clarke, was one of the earliest white men in the country. He came to Africa in 1890 at the age of seventeen, after he had contracted TB in England. Unless he went to live in a drier climate, his doctors told him, he would not last for more than three months. Almost from the moment he stepped off the boat in Africa his condition improved. Soon he was fit to undertake any job. While still a young man, he accompanied Cecil Rhodes to the *kraal* of Lobengula, chief of the Matabele in present-day Rhodesia. Lobengula turned to Rhodes and asked who this man was and for what crime he had left England. Not for any crime, Rhodes replied, but because he needed African *muti* (medicine). The old chief examined Clarke carefully and then commented that, just as the mopani was tall and straight, so also was he, and just as its core was hard, so also was his heart. Ever since then Clarke was called "Mopani."

Lobengula could not have been more right, but what he did not account for was Clarke's cleverness. Shortly after the meeting there was an outbreak of rinderpest in Lobengula's *kraal* and cattle began to die by the thousands. Clarke bought up all the carcasses for virtually nothing, skinned them and made biltong (like beef jerky) out of the meat. He sold the hides to traders at a vast profit and the dried meat he stored in sheds until the next famine when the Matabele were willing to pay the outrageous prices he demanded. Such was Clarke's beginning as a bush financier. In 1898 he founded the Bechuanaland Trading Association at the "Old Drift" on the Zambezi, seven miles from the present-day town of Livingstone. There he built the first hotel in Northern Rhodesia, making it his headquarters for a string of trading stores throughout the vast Barotse country to the west. One of his ventures was a ferry service across the Zambezi. At the price of three pennies per person he made a handsome profit for himself, until one day the river began to go down and the Africans discovered that they could save themselves the fare by crossing on foot. Almost overnight Clarke was out of business. But he was *not* going to be defeated: setting out into the bush he shot two antelope which he placed in the river near the ford. Within a day the place was swarming with crocodiles and once again he was back in business.

For many years Erica lived at Chikupi, one of her father's many farms. The lechwe were so plentiful, she remarked, that often she was forced to drive through a herd rather than waste many miles and sometimes hours driving around it. To set an example her father, who was a strict conservationist, refused to shoot game even for the pot. Erica followed his example, and one night she was awakened, she remembers, by a gunshot. She rushed out of the house to find that an eland had been poached by a

group of Afrikaans-speaking farmers. She brought out a
.22 rifle and, taking careful aim, shot one in the leg. The
poachers, who had assumed she would not mind losing one
eland, were astonished. She shouted to them that unless
they cleared off her farm immediately she was going to
aim for their private parts. They wasted no time in
leaving.

Erica told me that her present husband, Ronny Critchley, was the best husband she had ever had. "The other
ones were absolute bastards. I remember once I told one of
them that when he died I would do the Charleston on his
coffin." Critchley, her third husband, was a huge, tall man
who had been a colonel in the Thirteenth Hussars in India.
Once we had settled ourselves in the sitting room, he
mixed the drinks and prepared the kerosene lamps for the
evening. When he spoke, which was seldom, even Erica
was silent.

In the afternoon, after we had tea in porcelain cups, I
was introduced to the animals. There was Oliver, a duiker,
Lulu, the lechwe, who grazed on the front lawn, Venus, a
huge brown bush pig who grubbed his meals on the back
porch, and Dumdum, a baby hippo which weighed four
hundred pounds. Dumdum's mother had died after falling
into a hunter's trap. The police had brought the orphan to
the Critchleys in a Land Rover, and a special enclosure
and bath had been built for her near the house.

Every afternoon after tea the Critchleys examine their
herds of lechwe. We drove with them in their Land Rover
to the Luwoto River, a tributary of the Kafue. The treeless
country was covered with flattened grass — which looked
like motionless waves. Sparingly the Bell of Saint Mary,

*The wideness of her
plains has in it such
freedom and such
promise, that I myself,
who have been born
and bred by the sea,
and in Europe, find it
difficult to live away
from it, in Africa
never missed it.*

— *Isak Dinesen,*
Introduction to *Olive
Schreiner*, Story of
an African Farm

a delicate blue flower, protruded from the stalks. The lechwe, nervous herds of ochre-colored antelope, grazed in groups of several hundred near the river. They allowed us to approach within thirty yards of them. The males, who have lyre-shaped horns, were far more numerous than the females. Poachers, according to Erica, prefer the females to the males, since they are not as fierce and their skins are thicker. Six African game wardens are camped over the twenty-thousand-acre ranch, but still the poaching continues.

For the Critchleys there is something new every time they see the herds: seasons change, and the animals' temperaments fluctuate, according to whether they are breeding or foaling. Erica feels that since the lechwe used to exist over most of the country but now are limited to just a few areas on the Kafue Flats, it is her duty to protect them.

She knows the names of all the birds. On the edge of the reeds the black-winged stilt was doing a solitary dance near some pratincoles who were hawking insects in the reeds. On the water there was a mass of species: great white herons, marsh harriers, goliath herons, spur-winged geese, wood ibis, sacred ibis, African white pelicans and the red-billed skimmers, which flew inches above the water scooping crustaceans with their extended lower mandibles. Erica knew all the birds and to her it was a great compliment when the birds returned each year to her stretch of the river. When we arrived back at the house there was a mourning dove in the big fig tree. We both listened to its song and then Erica turned to me and said, her lips puckered and her right hand moving up and down as though she were beating out the rhythm of a song: "Somebody

lays one egg, somebody lays three, but I only lay two, two, two."

But there was business to attend to. While we had been away at the river a game warden had brought in a poacher. In his hand was the mummified head of a lechwe as evidence. The man, who was dressed in rags, did not seem to mind being caught. He assumed the attitude of someone who had stopped by for a visit. As soon as Erica saw the lechwe head in his hand, her face, once benign, compacted into a small tight display of lips and flaring nostrils. "You fornicating bastard," she yelled to him. She was on the verge of hitting the man, but at the last minute she kept her hands at her side. She issued orders to the warden to lock him up in the vervet monkey's cage and then imperiously strode over to the house.

After a few sips of her drink Erica changed. Her face had not lost its strength and anger but her voice had softened. She looked outside at the flat country half-lit by the moon and then back wistfully at the hissing pressure lamp on the table. Flying ants suicidally crashed into the glass and cockroaches, moths and crickets lay in a rude mess in spilt kerosene on the table. "All this fabulous wild life and bugger-all interest from the African. Without us Europeans, I doubt there would be a damn thing left. You know, American children know far more about African animals than do most Africans. You wouldn't believe it but the majority of blacks in the towns have never seen a wild animal. That's why we've built schools in the game reserves so they can identify an elephant or a hippopotamus. God knows, those who have seen an animal think of it only as bloody *nyama* (meat) like that bastard in Tango's cage." Erica illustrated her point by telling me an incident which had happened a few years before. "Once during the rains I was driving from Lusaka to the ranch when I came to a flooded river. The bridge spanning it was half under water. I crossed it on foot and decided that since I was in no particular rush to get to the other side I'd wait until the flood subsided before I drove the car across. There was a group of Africans also waiting to cross over. They walked up to the car and peered in the back to have a look at Sally, my pet lion. One of them asked me what sort of dog it was. 'No dog at all,' I replied. 'It's a lion.' Their jaws dropped and their eyes opened to their full size. For the rest of the night they refused to get within two hundred yards of the car."

On the day following our arrival, after the Critchleys had gone into Lusaka for supplies, two African policemen stopped at the ranch on a routine visit. I took them over to see the Critchleys' hippopotamus. Both policemen gazed at the sight of her half-submerged in the little pool of water. It was apparent they had never seen a hippopotamus before. Their conversation in a native dialect was filled with long breathless exclamations. Finally one of them turned to me and asked whether Dumdum, when she was older, would grow feathers. "Feathers?" I said to myself half in disbelief, half in wonder. Their question could well have been comic; yet it had disheartening implications. Erica was not surprised when I later told her the remark. She drew a dismal meaning from it. "It's the old story," she said, "you mustn't mind starting with bugger-all and after twenty years ending up with bugger-all. That's Africa for you; never a dull moment."

Near a desolate unguarded section of the Mozambique frontier is a government rest house called Kachalola. It sits high on a hill overlooking one of Zambia's bleakest regions. On the edge of the hill is the Great East Road, which joins Lusaka in the center of the country with Fort Jameson on the east. The road, a mass of holes, corrugations and hairpin bends, today is full of the noisy traffic of petrol tankers speeding toward the capital to avert a fuel shortage, since Zambia's only rail connection with the sea has been cut off and its flow of oil and petrol, so vital to it in this period of economic adolescence, has been stopped. In search of an alternative supply route the government has recruited an army of trucks and drivers to bring it in by road. Under this heavy load of machinery and fuel, the Great East Road, which was originally designed to carry only the occasional Land Rover and truck, has collapsed. Pits the size of manhole covers dot its surface, and the wrecks of trucks which could not negotiate the abrupt corners lie like skeletons along the road.

There is a bar in the rest house at Kachalola. Every evening before dusk it grows noisy with voices and the crackling sound of news broadcasts from England. Generally the locals, contract men who are working to build a new road, challenge visitors to dart games. It is a simple little ceremony which takes a short time, and usually the visitor loses and buys the drinks.

Here in the bar and along the crumbling road the new Africa challenges the old and wins. The whites, the blacks, the organic and the inorganic are all involved in progress: the road once used by wagons and horses now broken up by the incessant load of steel and petroleum, the old men of the villages clothed once in skins now dressed in uncomfortable trousers and jackets, and this bar which used to be loud with the voices of a rough swaggering group of men now filled with the unmodulated conversation of professional itinerants. Today, one place is like another, one face much the same as many. The old names and the spectacles of their lives are being rapidly forgotten.

Except: in a darkened corner of the bar there is an autographed picture of "Kachalola" Broomfield. It shows a distinguished-looking man dressed in a frayed three-piece tweed suit and sporting a well-trimmed beard and an enormous moustache (he always boasted that he could tie it behind his head). The eyes are squinting in the sun, the mouth is drawn into laughter and the chin, although not visible under the beard, is set far forward of his head.

"Kachalola" Broomfield is a man whose history would have been full of inaccuracies had it been written by him alone. Luckily there were others to record some of the incidents. He came to Rhodesia in 1892 at the age of forty-five, when most men think about settling down. His real name was Spencer but as a youth he had had it changed. He liked to refer to himself as a doctor and claimed that he had studied medicine at the University of Edinburgh, but in reality his doctorate was the result of a five-dollar correspondence course he once had taken. Soon after arriving in Rhodesia he was thrown into jail on charges of highway robbery and murder, but thanks to a horse which was conveniently waiting outside his cell, he managed to escape. He was again imprisoned, this time in Blantyre, British Central Africa (now Malawi), thereby acquiring the doubtful honor of being the first man in Central Africa to be arrested as the result of the telegraph. He was soon released, and after being deported from British Central Africa, he joined up with an expedition in Northern Rhodesia searching for gold. After a year he tired of this pastime and, in its place, took up the far more profitable occupation of robbing slave caravans. Even as late as the 1900's raiders brought slaves from the interior of the African continent to fill the households of wealthy Arabs. Once a slave caravan fell into Broomfield's hands he released the slaves and kept the goods and ivory for himself. When the slave trade ceased he took to elephant poaching. Whenever he was caught with a pair of tusks he always claimed that he was fulfilling his one-elephant-a-year allowance accorded him by his license. Once, however, Broomfield was caught with two pairs of tusks. Coincidentally the four pieces of ivory were each almost the exact same weight and size. He explained to the authorities that he had shot a freak four-tusked elephant and was released from jail. For several years afterward there was a blistering controversy among scientists over this supposed mutation.

Broomfield had a total of nine native wives, and in one district alone he is said to have left thirty-six half-caste children. One of his wives was once stolen by a European, and as soon as Broomfield discovered her missing he set chase and finally caught up with the abductor in a bar at Fort Jameson. He drew out his revolver and was about to shoot the man when spectators interceded and asked Broomfield to reconsider the matter over a drink. Broomfield had one, then another and still another. After several hours they had become close friends and the two men left the bar arm in arm to find Broomfield's wife. She, meanwhile, had heard about the trouble and had fled to another lover.

Broomfield bought his first wife from a hotelkeeper for two donkeys. The town's butcher said she was the most beautiful girl he had ever laid eyes on and that if he had owned three donkeys he would have bought her himself. Broomfield also had two European wives. One of them had come out to Rhodesia to marry another man and when she arrived the man told her that a marriage ceremony was not necessary in this country. When he heard this story

Her glance fell on us — she started visibly. She opened the cavity that sporadically served her as a mouth. Most of the ivory in Africa flashed into sight. "The hag's got lips like a pair of balloon tires," my son remarked scornfully. We drew nearer. Her cheery smile grew — and grew. It developed into a howl of laughter.
— Daniel W. Streeter,
Denatured Africa

Broomfield was so incensed that he beat up the man and married the woman on the spot. She died the next year and when, many years later, he decided to build a headstone for her grave, he could not remember her name.

When Broomfield was eighty-one years old he had his first tooth pulled. He went to a dentist in Lusaka and, refusing an anesthetic, calmly watched it being extracted. The charge was *10s. 6d.*, but Broomfield presented the dentist with a five-pound note and said, "Keep that. It was worth it." Just to prove that the other teeth were strong he stuck an elephant cartridge into his mouth and ripped the bullet out of its case.

For many years Broomfield had a farm at Mile 195 on the Great East Road, the present-day site of the Kachalola government rest house, which was named after him. He cultivated a variety of crops at different times during his career, but for him there was no attraction in remaining long in one spot. Whenever the farm was beginning to show a profit he disappeared into the bush on another one of his many schemes. Finally, in the early thirties, when Africa was becoming too civilized for him, he set sail for Australia and wandered about Arnheimland in the north, where he was found near death by a coastal schooner. He died not long afterward in the hospital at Darwin. The Africans who work at Kachalola and who remember him claim that they can still hear him calling for tea. None dare steal anything lest his ghost, which is tyrannical toward thieves, pursue them. Broomfield, who was certainly no paragon on matters of private property, has finally managed to achieve a vague and relative respectability.

The ghosts of the past we sensed in Kachalola pursued

us along the road to Fort Jameson. It seemed a generation of creators had passed this way before, but had not stayed long. When we drove into Fort Jameson, covered in dust, the spirit of the pioneers was now apparent. At noon upon our arrival a few half-dead dogs requisitioned the only available shade in town. Storefronts were boarded up and the streets which must once have been well kept were now fallen into a state of disrepair. A few Land Rovers were parked outside the Provincial Headquarters Building and in front of the Game Department Office, but they were official cars. All that remained of Fort Jameson were the local government officials and one or two stubborn farmers. Even for the Africans "Fort Jimmy," as it is called, was considered a dead end. If one wanted to succeed in politics or business this town was not the place.

Years before, Fort Jameson had been prosperous. In the 1880's and 90's when cattle were dying of rinderpest all over southern Africa the Luangwa Valley, fifty miles from Fort Jameson, was found to be free of this dread disease. The town soon began to prosper as a cattle-distributing center and drovers came in from as far north as German East Africa. But the prosperity soon turned sour, for in the 1920's the tsetse fly descended into the Luangwa Valley, endangering the lives of both cattle and men. Cotton was planted around Fort Jameson to take up the slack but within one season that was destroyed by an unknown disease. Burley tobacco was then planted and when it survived, Fort Jameson became once again the slick, busy town of former years, this time with a complement of three hundred farmers. There were bad years of course, but almost everyone was solvent to survive the disasters. However, by the 1940's and 50's a better quality tobacco was found to grow in Southern Rhodesia and almost overnight the market for Fort Jameson burley collapsed. Some farmers sensed what was going to happen in advance and sold their farms to unsuspecting buyers, but most of them waited until it was too late, only to discover that they were bankrupt. They fled to the homes of relatives and friends throughout Africa, where once again they could begin the long ponderous business of settling.

That night we stayed in a vacant farmhouse which once had witnessed the elusive prosperity of burley. Now the Game Department had taken it over to house their game guards. One room was filled with a coffinlike cage which contained a Gabon viper. All the rooms were denuded of their furniture. We chose the dining room to spend the night. It was heavy with the smell of mildew and when I opened one of the lead-paned windows, the cool night air did little to dislodge the odor.

In the morning when it was light I went outside to look at the house. The only trees that looked cared for were the jacarandas, but they were naturally neat trees. They cast a shadow of brilliant, almost cobalt blue, over the driveway. Four rotting wattle poles were all that was left of the entrance gate, although once a thatched roof had been suspended over them which now lay broken in little patches on the ground. On the left of the drive a pineapple orchard was covered with thorn bushes. The outline of an ornamental pond was still visible and even a few hardy water lilies floated on the surface of the water. Towering overhead was a stand of bamboo stalks, colored yellow and green with such precision that they looked as though they might once have been painted. Sculptured birdbaths had been left in the sunken garden in front of the house. They had turned green and lay between the faint outlines of the flower beds. The brick-and-thatch house still protected a clump of tired bougainvillea and shaded a frangipani tree. Each room was paneled in dark wood, and the living room was separated from the veranda by white arching columns. The lime wash on the walls of the kitchen had flaked off; the room had been taken over by the family of one of the game guards. Cooking, eating and sleeping were now done on the floor. The owners of the house would have cared once. They had lived in the house for thirty years, planted six thousand acres of tobacco, and had been very particular about how they lived. One night after their six thousand acres had become valueless they packed all their belongings into a five-ton truck and drove away for good.

There are a few Europeans in Fort Jameson who remember the past. Les Allen, the head of the Game Department, knows some of the old names although he himself has only been in Fort Jameson for two years. Old "Ma" Jerominsky, he told me, is one of the few left. Her husband, "old Jerry," was a farmer-cum-poacher, the usual combination of professions in Fort Jameson during the old days. After many years of leading a solitary life he decided to marry. As there were few marriageable women in Northern Rhodesia he wrote to the mayor of his native town in Germany and asked him to select a pretty, hard-working bride for him. The mayor wrote back to say that one had been chosen and that she was making preparations to sail to Africa. On the long-awaited day of her arrival in Africa Jerominsky rode to the coast to meet her. The woman who presented herself to him however did not resemble the one whose picture he had been sent. Instead of a finely shaped woman, this one was heavy-featured and rough. She explained to Jerominsky that her cousin, who had been the mayor's choice, had at the last minute decided against the plan and allowed her to go in her place. Jerominsky examined the woman's teeth, walked around her several times and then said to her: "Hell, you are no beauty, but after all a woman is a woman, so you better come along. Besides I've already paid five pounds for the license." The marriage was a complete success, although Jerominsky refused to admit it. For many years he had a buffalo which was allowed to roam freely about the farm. After several years it attacked Mrs. Jerominsky. Jerry refused to do anything about it until it later attacked his pedigreed bull. He thereupon shot it and explained, "I could get another wife for the same price as the last one: nothing. But the bull cost me four hundred pounds."

Buck and Cass Sayers were contemporaries of Jerry. They lived outside Fort Jameson and, later, near Fort Manning. Once when they had a woman and her child staying at their farm the D.C. received a note saying, "Mrs. L's child has convulsions, please send bottle of whiskey." He wrote back that his wife said whiskey was not good for convulsions and later received an answer which read, "Cass has been bitten by a snake, please send bottle of whiskey." The D.C. replied, "My wife says that by the time the runner gets back Cass will be either dead or recovered; in either case whiskey will not be necessary."

Norman Carr also survives. We met him in his office after lunch. He sat down on the back seat of a car which was lying on the floor and drew out a small pipe which he puffed on intermittently. Carr spoke only when it was absolutely essential, expressing his thoughts not through words but through gestures and expressions. He had once been in the Game Department here at Fort Jameson, but since then he has formed his own hunting firm which operates in the concessions along the edges of the game reserve. He was born in the bush and had during his youth walked over most of the game country in Northern Rhodesia. He was well dressed: his khaki trousers were newly pressed, his bush jacket had been starched and his neck was enclosed in a maroon cravat. For him appearances were important: they generated respect and respect in the bush was as important at times as a gun. Every word was calculated to command and to describe, nothing more. "Yes," he said, "I think I remember you. You were with the chap who went to see my lions." More than likely he had not remembered me. He merely wanted to drop the matter. The lions were, after all, dead. Their story, like most of the past, was not important. Just memories, and memories must be discarded for the sake of efficiency and sometimes for peace. Some other time when he was older and leisure was all he had left he might look back, but now the most important matter was "getting on with it."

So he stretched his legs out on the hard concrete floor and stared at me because I happened to be in his line of vision. His face had not changed since I first met him. The lines might have gotten a little deeper and his eyes might have faded slightly, but his manner was no different from the time he walked out of the Game Department Office to examine some poached ivory and to see what we wanted. He introduced himself and after listening to our request he agreed to let us see his lions, on the condition that we approached them in the company of Nelson, his game guard. The lions had not hurt anybody yet, but they could easily kill a man if they chose to do so.

Of course Carr was right: when Nelson released them from their cage and they padded toward us they looked as though they could kill a man with little difficulty. They were the size of miniature ponies and their manes made their heads stand out from the rest of their bodies. Their purrings ran through their necks and stomachs and legs and seemed to emanate from the inside of the earth. I ran my fingers through one of their manes and remember feeling a cluttering of thorns and ticks. Once Big Boy, the mildest-mannered of the two, for a brief second closed his teeth around my hand. They were heavy like pointed hammers and although they clamped onto me very gently they left white marks on my skin.

In the afternooon we walked along the Luangwa River to search for rhino and much later, when our mouths were sticky and our legs bleeding from the thorns, we returned to the camp. The lions, who had been confined to their cage in the afternoon, had vaulted the ten-foot barricade and were now resting on the sandbar in the river. We watched George, one of the members of our party, walking toward them. Suddenly when he reached the lions' territory, Little Boy, as though convulsed by a primeval instinct, sprang to his feet. George removed his hat, a wide-brimmed arrangement, and held it poised in his hand. The game guard swore at the lion and it hesitated momentarily to look at him. But by then it was on George: its two massive paws on his shoulders and its head level with his. George calmly swatted it with his hat and then, like Androcles after he had been recognized by the lion, calmly turned his back on it and returned to us.

Norman Carr had deliberately forgotten about the lions because shortly after we saw them they killed a girl in a

Many years ago a man and his wife were looking for butterflies in Uganda. A game warden saved them from getting a "nasty scare" by a lion. The wife said to her husband: "Timothy, you lost a lovely specimen." The game warden broke in and said to her: "Madame, if I had not been there, you would have lost one too."

— Told to me by James Manley

village not far from the spot where we had first seen them. Carr, as a result, sent them to one of the remote parts of the Luangwa. Now, he presumed, they must be dead. He sucked at his pipe and looked at me as though he wished that I would drop the matter. The lions were now just a memory which he did not care to discuss. Far more important were his present plans to develop the Luangwa Valley for tourists. He ran hunting safaris, special walking safaris, and he had leased one of the lodges in the park. He inquired whether I had been to the Luangwa on this visit. If not, I would certainly be surprised at the amount of game. "Far superior to most African game parks," he said. "Like going back to the Stone Age."

On the following day we met Johnny Uys, the game warden, on the steel barge which carried our Land Rover across the Luangwa into the game reserve. After being introduced, he mentioned that there was a bush fire in the northwestern part of the park. He was taking out a few men in the afternoon to see whether it had caused much damage. He said it might be a long uncomfortable ride but there was no telling what we might see. Would we care to join him?

We left our car at his office and drove with him to his house which was nicknamed the "mushroom" since the second story was larger than the ground floor. The roof commanded a view of the Luangwa crawling through the balding countryside. Near the house the river was dry and its bed had hardened into a cribbage board of elephant and buffalo spoor. Across from us a puku antelope whistled to warn trespassers of the boundaries of its territory. Uys had heard the same sound many times yet he paused to listen once again.

We drove fast with the vents open to allow the warm air to cool our faces. There was little game to be seen in the middle of the day — the occasional Burchell's zebra, a Thornycroft's giraffe and a Lichtenstein hartebeest (both common only to the Luangwa), pukus and impala. There were gray-hooded kingfishers near the river and once when we stopped I heard a golden-tailed woodpecker peppering a tree. Occasionally the copper-brown monotony of the bush was shattered by the lilac-breasted roller. It never failed to relieve the monotony of the country with its flash of sea-blue. But otherwise there was never a break from the brachiastegia forests. The ground was littered with dead leaves and branches and the trees were lifeless contortions. We stopped on the Kapamba River at a geologist's camp. Samples were spread over a table and a geological map covered a reed wall. The geologist tried to evade the question of what he was prospecting for. His assistant, a boy just out of school in England, sat in a corner never uttering a word. He was suffering from sunburn and was in agony. Ten miles further on we drove into the camp of another geologist. He and his wife were living in a section of the bush which had been swept by fire. He gave Uys two elephant tusks which one of his boys had found. Over the static of a radio we could hear the geologist's wife splashing inside a tin bathtub. She called for us to stay for tea, but Uys replied that we were in a hurry to find the fire by nightfall.

Uys deftly maneuvered along the faint track, occasionally detouring around fallen trees into the spear grass. Although his eyes never left the bush he did most of the talking. He spoke of the value of bush fires, of the early burns just after the rains which replace the long grass with new green shoots, and of the late burns which convert the forests into plains and allow more grazing animals to live off the bush. He spoke of the nutrients that the bush can provide, not only for animals but also for men. "Famine relief is a farce," he said. Africans, he explained, need never go hungry even in the sparsest country. There is always food to be found. Uys had spent most of his life tramping the country on foot and whenever he exhausted his supply of ammunition he killed rats, mice and moles by placing snare traps in front of their holes. He gave me a piece of wild fruit to eat, a shriveled brown papery thing devoid of taste which, according to Uys, had great nutritional value. In the dry bed of the Lunjovu River, Uys dug a hole. It soon began to fill with thin trickles of water, fresh and cool and far more refreshing than the beer which had been lying on the hot floor plates of the Land Rover. On the bank of the river Uys broke off a branch of *musamba*, peeled off the bark, and made the core into a strong rope. He took this sinewy piece of pulp and coiled it around the thin branch of the *ci nyé nyé*. Removing the branch he put the core, now in the shape of a circle, to his lips and blew. The noise was a bleating sound like that of a sheep or the whistle of a nightjar. Although we did not wait to prove the matter, Uys claims that the sound is an exact imitation of the cry a young duiker antelope makes when it is calling for help. The females of that species are roused by the sound and when they come to assist, the natives trap them.

Uys had lived to be a specialist of the bush. He knew his country better than any man, and, in it, every tree, rock and animal by both their Latin and their native names. He knew how and why they existed and how each one could help him survive. In the early morning he reads scientific journals, making notations in the columns and writing down information in a notebook. He corresponds with ecologists and botanists and has himself written for wildlife journals and become known in the scientific world as an authority on the Luangwa Valley and on the Kafue Game Reserve, where he was once stationed. Although he never went to school beyond Standard 5 (fifth grade), the world of science and exactitude is not alien to him. After having spent a lifetime in the bush he feels that the only way to continue submitting himself to it is by understanding it in the realms beyond intuition. It is a character which, on first appraisal, does not seem to suit him.

His parents were South African. In 1902, following the Boer defeat at the hands of the British, they packed all their belongings and trekked with an ox wagon north to find new lands. Uys's mother was related to "Oom Paul" Krueger, a fact attested to by the old family Bible which today lies in the Voortrekker Monument near Pretoria. Once a year on Dingaan's Day a ray of light beams through a crack in the lofty edifice and splashes the worn book with sunlight.

Uys's father first settled in Southern Rhodesia but he found the presence of the British intolerable. Finally, in 1904 he reached Northern Rhodesia, an unsettled country, where he intended to live as he and his ancestors before him had lived. He tried farming but after a time he took up other jobs. For many years he carted bales of copper from the mines in the north to a railhead. It was hard work and kept him away from home for weeks at a time.

Uys inherited his father's distaste for the British. He feels that if he understands any race it is the African.

When he was young, he remembers, the African was trustworthy. There was no risk, he said, in sending one off with an envelope containing pound notes, for it was always safely delivered. But the British, he feels, destroyed that happy situation. They broke the man-to-man trust. They did nothing for the country besides putting pants on those who had before been quite happy to live in a state of nakedness. They failed to build any roads in the country until the 1950's. The game parks, which apart from the copper were the country's greatest resource, were totally neglected. According to Uys, employment in the Game Department was made as unattractive as possible. Starting pay for an African policeman was twenty pounds while a game guard began with a mere nine pounds.

For twenty-two years Uys worked for the British government. He began with a monthly salary of £12. 6s. for building roads, and after suffering two bouts of blackwater fever he went to work for the Game Department. He believes that the concept of conservation was continually ignored by the British. Only one Governor in the history of Northern Rhodesia ever visited a game park, and then his aim was to fish. Poachers were given minimal sentences and treated leniently. One Governor, in fact, advised a convicted poacher to continue poaching. The British, the "home-born bastards," as Uys calls them, treated him and all the other "local baboons" as though they were not fit for their society.

In the old days, Uys continued, the Afrikaaner storekeeper, who was barely able to write his name, maintained a credit system which was based exclusively on honor. There were no accounts; each customer remembered what he owed and paid it when he could. The old storekeeper would turn to Uys and say, "Your conscience will hurt you, Johnny, if you don't pay." Always debts were honored but the British, according to Uys, have broken the faith. They have not been loyal to the men who worked for them. When they severed their ties with Northern Rhodesia after Independence they dissolved all their debts and promises to those who had served their administration. It is as though they were ashamed of their past and were trying to make amends with the new order by refusing to recognize their former allies.

Today the government's attitude to the game department has been reversed, according to Uys. The African government has taken a positive interest in the parks. In Zambia's two years of self-rule, Dr. Kaunda, the Prime Minister, has visited the Luangwa Game Reserve three times and has publicly announced that if Uys has any problems with government officials he should speak directly to him. In addition, the Parks Department is today working with a budget six times the one allotted to it under the British. "If these game parks still remain as well stocked with animals in a hundred years as they are today," Uys said, "the only people who will deserve the credit for it will be this African government."

The word "African," has come to mean a black man, but Uys applies it to himself. His roots are in the bush with the African's. His game guards are men of the old school: unread, tough, resourceful and obedient. They regard him as their commander. He, in turn, treats them as his soldiers. He is fierce with them when they misconstrue his orders and protective of them against outsiders. They are "his men" and he is responsible for them at all times. He is a hard taskmaster but their reward is the honor which his command showers upon them.

The more that men like myself who have enjoyed nearly forty years of sunshine and happiness in Africa support the new order which has replaced the old, the sooner the country will smile again.

— *Sir Michael Blundell,*
So Rough a Wind

I would not be able to guess how many times my car has gotten stuck on a rainy night down the road and the Africans got out of their beds and gave us a push, joking the whole time. I can assure you I would not have been able to do the same.

— *From a conversation with a coffee planter on the slopes of Mount Kilimanjaro*

Africans, Uys maintains, are not lazy. White people are inclined to judge their lassitude as idleness. On the contrary, Uys says, they are doing what all members of the animal kingdom do: they are conserving their energy. Most of the day, for instance, lions lie drowsily in the shade, but when they are stalking they have in readiness a vast stockpile of energy. During the final charge their muscles are like steel. "Just so with the African," Uys said. "Most of the day he may sit around on his bottom looking into space but when he is called upon to do something which requires energy he can be a virtual powerhouse. It's one of nature's mechanisms designed to cope with the hot and uncomfortable environment."

An African, Uys maintains, is territory-conscious, particularly in the sphere of human relations. When he meets a European for the first time he will start testing him to see how many liberties he may take. If he is working for the European he might begin by feigning laziness to see if his employer will tolerate such behavior. Once he has satisfied himself, he ceases to play the game. He can now proceed in full knowledge of the other person's power and the limits of his influence.

Uys has a boyish face which can register surprise, anger and happiness in quick succession. Like a caged animal which paces in front of the bars of its cage, he harbors a violent energy which waits to be released. When he believes in something, he believes in it to the limits of his energy. Survival has taught him to be complete and at the same time confident. He maintains that unless men try to understand wild things they will not be able to understand themselves. He seems continually to try to test the power

that lurks behind the bars of his personality, and though
he can hardly find its presence comforting, he never fails to
use it to maintain his authority as a leader. I learned that
he has given orders for his body to be left in the bush when
he dies so that it can be eaten by the hyenas and jackals.

We drove through the afternoon stopping only to stand
on the hood of the car to look for the bush fire. We reached
it just before dark: a thin band of flames slowly gouging
out a path of blackened earth. Stopping only briefly we determined its position so a fire-fighting crew could locate
it in the morning. The drive back was in darkness. Uys
pointed out and identified trees and plants which were
hardly visible. Whenever a buck stood in the road ahead of
us transfixed by the lights of the car, Uys turned them off
momentarily to give the animal a chance to dash away.
The bush seemed to be alive that night; eyes shone in the
darkness and occasionally a patch of shadow would erupt
with a clattering of hooves.

We stayed at Mfuwe in the Luangwa Valley for almost
a week. In the mornings I was awakened by the yawn-
ings and belchings of a family of hippos in the river. Often
before breakfast we drove to distant parts of the reserve to
watch the game. Once we were locked in the stamping and
beating of a herd of four hundred buffalo and another time
we crept up to an elephant close enough to hear the rumblings of his stomach. On several unsuccessful occasions
we sought the White Lady, an albino impala which has
been seen fleetingly for the past eight years. In the after-
noons everyone slept. The rains had not yet come and the
air was heavy with languor. No one slept very well and at
four when we reappeared to take our tea we looked slow-
witted and cursed the weather.

The evenings were loud. Most of the visitors went to bed soon after dinner and left the bar to the elephant croppers and the game wardens. Once Stewart Campbell, a huge, bearded ex-soldier who had fought with Mike Hoare in the Congo, walked into the bar dressed in nothing but a turban made from a towel and recited a passage from *Othello*. Johnny Uys then stood on the trunk of a Borassus palm and declaimed sixty verses of "Eskimo Nell." Everyone had a specialty: an imitation of Louis Armstrong singing "Hello, Dolly," a soft-shoe act on the bar or an unusual capacity for beer. At twelve o'clock the bar closed but it was reopened almost immediately to allow the party to continue. When the game wardens left, just before dawn, they merely washed and then proceeded to their bush offices. To miss a good drinking session for the sake of sleep is a sacrilege to one's manhood.

The Luangwa Valley is divided into northern and southern parts. Only the southern is open to visitors; the other, being devoid of roads, can be reached by a long and difficult foot safari through tsetse-ridden country. The only people who know it are game wardens and poachers. Between the two parks is a narrow strip of country called the Munamazi Corridor, through which a crude track was recently made by the Game Department. For over a hundred and twenty miles it wanders through the bush until on the southern end, it reaches the Luangwa and, on the northern, it joins the Great North Road. Not over twenty cars a year drive over it from one end to the other.

Africa being the way it is, we did not reach the Munamazi Corridor on the day we left the lodge. A faulty carburetor delayed us for several hours and once it had been repaired we had to wait for a ferry landing to be constructed before we could proceed any further. As soon as we reached the other side of the river I drove off the road to look for a camping site and came to a neat collection of reed huts. A European was sitting in a lookout post on the river. He waved us over to him and within minutes he had invited us to have dinner with him and to spend the night. He was an old man. His skin was waxy and speckled with faded freckles, and his eyes were heavy with water. He sat in a tattered canvas chair with a pair of binoculars and a bottle of whiskey beside him. "I've been watching that *pickanin* [little] elephant all day," he said. "It doesn't seem to want to leave the river. There must be something wrong with it." He had never left his chair since early morning. It was as though he was trying to relive one long melodious memory by watching the elephants coming down to water. He knew many by sight and told me their histories during the last few weeks. When he began to conjure up the past, he became blurry. Sometimes he related long lists of unrelated events, sometimes unconnected references to the things around him. He had killed too many elephants to recall how he had killed one in particular. Time, for him, did not pass in minutes and hours, but in years and decades. "In the twenties . . ." he would say.

His father had worked in the mines in South Africa — a suitable job for a father but not fit for him. At an early age he decided to devote his life to poaching and went to Northern Rhodesia for that purpose. Four years after he arrived in that country he reached the Luangwa Valley. At that time the valley was untouched by anyone save men of his profession. "I saw Africa as it used to be," he told me,

People feel so damned lonely, they need company, they need something bigger, stronger, to lean on, something that can really stand up to it all. Dogs aren't enough; what we need is elephants . . .

— *Romain Gary,*
The Roots of
Heaven

"but only the tail end. When I came here I really stuck my neck out. I arrived with one rifle and a string of porters whom I could not communicate with since I didn't know the language. But I caught on fast and made a few pennies off the ivory. I've always fancied this country particularly where the bush is thick. Sometimes when you round a corner you run smack into a rhino. Never a dull moment."

In 1938 the Game Department was formed and since he knew the valley better than anyone else he was appointed warden. During World War II he was the only white man throughout the valley. "When I set off from Fort Jameson I had one bottle of whiskey with me which I promised to share with the first white man I saw. I didn't touch it for four years."

When I awoke in the morning a herd of elephants had come and gone, leaving only the half-forgotten sound of their splashing. I peered out of the hut where I had spent the night and saw a bee eater flashing like a red spark along the banks of the river. Nearby a pack of vervet monkeys scuttled to the water's edge, their sentries scrutinizing the countryside from perches high in the brachiastegia.

After breakfast the old man returned to his binoculars and his bottle of whiskey. When we were about to leave he briefly turned away from the river and said, "You know, I don't think that elephant is well. It just won't leave the river and I dare say it's getting weaker." The old man was genuinely concerned with the fate of that one creature although in his lifetime he had killed many. Each year he still purchases an elephant license and ever since he retired from the Game Department he has managed to shoot an animal whose tusks were large enough to defray the license's cost. But, he admits, that is merely a tradition and

for him there is very little sport left in killing. His greatest
pleasure is merely living in the company of the great
beasts. It is a re-creation of the long stalks of his youth.

Not far from the old man's camp there is a grave. It lies
on an uncluttered plain near a baobab tree and bears the
name of W. Sayer, who was one of the Cockney brothers
who gained notoriety around Fort Jameson and Fort Manning because of his whiskey bouts. A tuskless elephant
had apparently charged him from behind. His porters
buried him on the spot where he died and years later a
headstone was placed on it. Sayer is one of the many who
have been killed while hunting in the Luangwa Valley.
J.B. Yule, another one mauled by an elephant, was one of
the few who had had some time to reflect before he died.
He penciled a note to his old friend "Bobo" Young, the
District Commissioner of Chinsali, saying "Dear Bobo, I
have got caught at last, going home this time. Ta-ta —
J.B. Yule."

Twenty miles from the old man's camp we drove onto
the Chibimbi pontoon, a short metal barge pulled across
the Luangwa by three lean Africans. It was a precarious
crossing since waves slapped against the front and the
back of the Land Rover, which extended over the barge's
extremities. On the far side of the river, tracks led in every
direction. We drove at a right angle from the river and
after several detours came to a track which seemed to have
been used more than the rest. The country was full of
people. As soon as they heard the car they ran out of their
huts to gaze at us and our belongings. It was uncommon
for them to see white people and particularly a white
woman. They laughed at Mary Anne, touched her clothes
and pulled her hair.

*Tell you of many a
hunter
Who facing a charge
has stood
And died, as a white
man should
Giving his life for
others,
Playing the game to
the end.
Tell me what death
can be better
Than dying to save a
friend.*

*— E. L. Mills,
East African
Professional Hunters
Association*

Twenty-five miles from the ferry we came to Chief Nabwalya's village, the traditional center of the surrounding native community. We had heard from the Game Department in Fort Jameson that an American ecologist and his wife, Stuart and Martha Marks, were living here. He was studying the relation between human populations and animal populations and had chosen Nabwalya because it was made up of a people oriented to hunting.

That was all I knew of Marks, but when he stepped out of his mud-walled hut I expected someone older. He was very young, working for his Ph.D. and with a sense of mission which I suppose had been inherited from his father, a missionary in the Congo. His wife had a lilting southern grace in her language and her walk.

There were no comforts in Nabwalya. Water had to be brought by hand from the river, one mile away. A bath was considered the supreme luxury. Their food was of the humblest variety. That which did not come out of tins was shot by Marks with his single-barreled shotgun given to him by the Game Department. For them there was little contact with other white people, as they had few visitors, and since they did not own a radio, no news from the outside world. Unlike most white people in Africa, they did their own housework and cooking as they believed the presence of a houseboy would have disrupted their study. They did not have any liquor, not because they were abstemious, but because bottles would break on the rough pitted road.

But they had learned to live with these discomforts. Their one anxiety was the unhealthy climate of Nabwalya. The decaying remains of a government outstation built in 1910 stand nearby on a hill as a reminder to Europeans of the hazards of this disease-ridden valley. The Marks, of course, had an advantage over the early officials since they were taking malaria prophylactics, something unknown in 1910, but there was still no certain means of preventing bilharzia, blackwater fever, hookworm and sleeping sickness. The rains were due shortly and then it would be impossible for them to leave the valley unless they chose to slog by foot through the treacle-thick mud. Since the nearest hospital was a five days' walk from Nabwalya there would be little chance of getting medical attention. It was not a pleasant thought for them, one which they tried not to talk about. On the following day they were going to drive to Mpika and then to Lusaka to buy supplies and prepare themselves for the rains.

Marks poaches with the Africans. He does so with the blessing of the Game Department, which has promised him that if he is caught by one of their game guards he will immediately be released. Since poaching is the tribe's principal means of supplying themselves with food it is important for him to understand every aspect of it. Marks told me that "there is a gap of misunderstanding about game conservation between these people and the Game Department. It makes no sense for them to protect animals which for them have only one purpose — to be killed for food. The whole theory of game protection has been developed by an affluent society. These people, unlike you and me, can't play games with their next meal." What might come of his study, he hopes, is for the Game Department to change its policy about poaching in order to adhere more strongly to native customs and requirements.

Since their chairs were broken we had lunch sitting on jerricans. The temperature rose to 105 degrees in the shade and sweat flowed in a continual stream down our faces. It was as uncomfortable and tiring to be idle as it was to be active. After lunch, we put on our hats and trekked to the Munamazi River, a mile from their camp. All along the way there were bare fallow fields soon to be put to the plow. The villagers will move away from their permanent homes and until the harvests they will live in the small temporary huts built along the borders of these fields. Apart from their muzzle-loaders a hut is their most important protection from wild animals. In the day no one need fear anything but at night every door is barred.

Along the river naked children were netting fish. We climbed a ridge and passed the foundations of the abandoned outstation which was now being used to house the small tin huts of the game guards. At the foot of the hill there was a series of hot mineral springs in which a hunchback was washing in an attempt to cure himself of his infirmity. All along the way Marks made notations of the game in an effort to make a census of the animal populations. We saw few animals, as most of them had learned to be wary of men. Wart hogs raced away at a distance of a hundred yards and all we ever saw of antelope were their hindquarters. We walked through balding bush for another two miles and came to a huge boulder-strewn cone called Kapili-Ndozi or the Hill of the Witches. It is a tradition among the Babisa people that criminals are left here to die. There were no human bones to be found, although we did discover the bleached femur of a buffalo. On our return to the Marks' camp we came upon a flock of guinea fowl. Marks set off in chase and for several minutes all we could see of him was his peaked hat bobbing up and down on the far side of bushes. Then his shotgun bellowed and he began to run. I joined in the chase but, unfortunately, the wounded bird vanished. Marks had one shell left so he decided to continue after the bird, allowing us to return to camp. A few minutes later we heard the report of his gun and he soon joined us with a guinea fowl hanging from his belt. The two of us cleaned and gutted it and then sat down with glasses of water to relieve the agony of our thirst.

We ate before it grew dark since kerosene for the lights was scarce. The guinea fowl was tough but no one mentioned it. Mrs. Marks prepared *insima*, corn ground up into a fine white powder and made into a gluey paste, which we dipped into a heavy brown gravy. Marks warned me that I must not say Game Department in the presence of the villagers as they might assume that he was in some way connected with it. The people of Nabwalya have a deep-rooted contempt for game officials. Marks had to renounce his association with them to ensure that his intentions in Nabwalya were not misconstrued by the inhabitants. We referred to the Game Department as "G.D." and couched any direct references to it in ambiguity.

Soon after dark Marks was bitten by a centipede. He mumbled to his wife that there was something crawling about in his shoe and when he took it off a long shiny black insect crawled out. Marks did not think he would suffer any ill effects from the wound, but as a precaution he cut an incision in the wound and sucked off the blood.

The alarm clock sounded at four. It had not been a pleasant night for I had slept on the hard ground inside the hut. Rats, they warned me, might chew my sleeping bag, but instead of rats an invasion of ants trekked across my face. Throughout the night we heard the hyenas howling on the outskirts of the village. In a distant part of the community drums were beaten almost constantly to scare the animals away.

We packed the car in darkness and with little delay we set off. The road was even worse than before. Marks and his wife drove ahead of us and stopped frequently to make notations of the game. At one point in the trip we saw a long line of elephants, like paper cutouts, walking south along the horizon. Across the Chifungwe Plain we counted a herd of six hundred buffalo. They thundered off when they saw us, leaving a solitary rhino grazing on a bush like a derelict steam engine.

Finally after four hours of driving we left the valley. We climbed a steep track up the escarpment and reached the top where the air was cooler. The atmosphere was still thick and cloying with the expectancy of rain, but here we could breathe without effort. We were in a more tolerable, familiar world. We stood and peered out at the land fifteen hundred feet below us. It was flat and empty from this altitude. To the north, lost in the smoke haze, it joined other valleys and formed the Great Rift, a geological nerve center running the length of Africa and as far north as the Dead Sea in the Near East.

Not far from where we climbed up onto the plateau we came to Mpika, a small town where trucks bringing petrol from Tanzania are repaired. Here there is an administrative center which dates back to the early years of the colony. Near the original D.C.'s house there is a small graveyard set in a cool grove of creepers and dead leaves. Rows of brick mounds support the fading headstones. Already the effects of erosion are making some of the inscriptions difficult to read. Most of the grave markers tell of deaths

from black water, malaria and sleeping sickness and of
men found by travelers as rotting corpses in their outsta-
tions. There are a few exceptions. On one grave lie two
bent airplane propellers, doubtlessly placed there by the
dead man's friends in a maudlin gesture to explain to
others the circumstances of his death. Next to him lies
Charles Lindsay Ross. On the gravestone is inscribed:

ELEPHANT

CONTROL OFFICER

BORN AT PORT PIRIE

SOUTH AUSTRALIA

15TH MAY 1877

KILLED BY HIS

350TH ELEPHANT

IN KAMWENDO'S COUNTRY

29TH MAY 1938

On his grave lie the decaying bones of his last elephant. A
year before he died he lost the use of one of his eyes. Simply by switching his gun from his right to his left shoulder
he was able to continue hunting. Like most professionals,
he eventually overplayed his hand: he attempted to hunt
while he was suffering from malaria. His arm was shaky
and after he made one inaccurate shot at an elephant the
beast turned around and killed him. There is a legend
around Mpika that for one week after his death the elephant which had killed him returned each night to stamp
on his grave. The District Commissioner finally shot the
animal and, as a reminder of Ross's unfortunate death, he
placed its skull on the ground over his casket. Ever since

then the grave has been unmolested. The skull has decayed considerably and within a few years I should think there will be nothing left.

Africa's colonial history is full of builders. Those who are remembered today are chiefly the ones who built nations and empires out of what was once an uncivilized continent. There were others, whose lives were on a smaller scale, who built houses to satisfy within themselves an innate sense of empire building. Had they been given the job of building an empire they would surely have done it with great expansiveness, but since they were not in that position they constructed bizarre and fantastic buildings. In Zambia alone there are at least ten of these extraordinary edifices as tokens of the unique personalities which the country once attracted. As late as 1947 a mammoth rest house was constructed by a District Commissioner who wished to celebrate the fact that he had once studied architecture in Germany. In the early days a pioneer by the name of "Chirapula" Stevenson constructed a house out of stone and rough wood and named it Stonehenge. In order to save plumbing expenses the toilet was built overhanging the moat. A close friend of Chirapula's called Ginger Dick followed his example and built a four-storied castle for himself. The structure was of a unique design and defied many laws of architecture. A door on the third floor was intended to connect the house with a proposed wing. Ginger Dick later built another house which resembled a Roman villa and contained a large sunken bathtub. He miscalculated the level of the water supply so whenever the plug was pulled out, instead of draining, the tub filled with water.

North of Mpika stands the most formidable of these creations. It is a cavernous Renaissance-style villa called Shiwa Ngandu, built and maintained along feudal lines by Sir Stewart Gore-Browne. It supports a native community which lives in mud-walled huts and small stone houses. As a part of this human complex there is a hospital, a post office, a school and a chapel. Once the estate supported a thousand men; today there are only sixty.

In the evening when we arrived the house was a huge ghostly shadow, the only lights in it being the imperfect reflections of the moon on the windows. Behind the house a huge granite outcrop called Nachipal, the Bald Man, loomed. Far down the hill on which the house was set glimmered the waters of Shiwa Ngandu, the Lake of the Royal Crocodile, where David Livingstone's little dog Chitane was drowned over a hundred years ago.

Sir Stewart was in bed when we arrived. We sat in an enclosed garden with his daughter and son-in-law and after dinner were led through stone passages covered in tapestries and along a balcony which faced onto a courtyard lit by flickering torches. In the bedroom the covers of the bed were turned down and a kerosene lamp was hissing on the bedside table. The walls were covered in pen-and-ink scenes of the canals of Venice.

In the morning I wandered through the gardens. Roses, frangipani and bougainvillea, growing in semi-disorder, covered every inch of ground. A row of stately eucalyptus trees bordered a road leading to the bell tower, which was once used to summon the workers from the fields. The garden followed the contours of the uneven country. From whatever angle I chose the house was impressive and bizarre. Even in England it would have been an extravaganza. The walls were indiscriminately covered with porches and gargoyles, and many windows were enclosed with iron railings. The addition of wings had evidently come to signify the passage of time, for it seemed there were as many of them as there had been years since the building's construction. The structure was covered with turrets, enclosed bridgelike corridors and iron latticework. What it lost in the absence of grace and power it gained through bulk.

Sir Stewart appeared from the front door. With him was his manservant Henry, who has been employed at Shiwa Ngandu for thirty-seven years. Sir Stewart, who had not had visitors for a few weeks, was delighted at the opportunity to show someone around the house. He ushered us into the sitting room, pointed out the Queen Anne desk and the portrait of Dame Ethel, his aunt, and then showed us the state dining room.

The dining room reminded me of a story I had once heard about Sir Stewart. At the beginning of the century when he was a young man Sir Stewart fell in love with a woman of extraordinary beauty. He pursued her relentlessly but when he asked her to marry him she refused. Years later, after she had married someone else, he fell in love with her daughter, who shared her mother's charm and beauty. Sir Stewart married her and took her off to his home in Africa. It was a lonely life for her, and when after many years the isolation began to tell, she left Sir Stewart and returned to England. In those few years that she was at Shiwa Ngandu it is said she stopped at nothing to relieve her boredom. Sir Stewart and Lady Gore-Browne entertained frequently and often on these occasions she wore costumes for her amusement. One of their guests from the 1930's told me he remembers patiently standing in the dining room with the other guests, all dressed in formal attire, waiting for their hostess, whom up to that point they had not seen. A hush pervaded the room as the minutes ticked by. Finally the French doors swung open and in walked Lady Gore-Browne dressed as Anne Boleyn and accompanied by two small Africans draped in red velvet and swinging enormous fans. She curtsied gracefully and then took her seat as though nothing could be more normal.

Sir Stewart ushered us into the library which was paneled in native wood and contained books on every subject. Above the mantel were the words *Ille terrarum mihi super omnes anculus ridet* ("This corner of the earth smiles on me more than any other place"). In one corner was a glass showcase which held his family medals. "This one," he said, pointing to a colorful pendant, "was won by my great-uncle." A friend of his once commented on its ornateness, "What strange bird has alighted on your shoulder?"

Sir Stewart explained to us that as a youth he had had no intention to settle in Africa. He first wanted to join the navy but he was disqualified on grounds of poor eyesight. He thereupon entered service in the army for the purpose of fighting the Boers. While he was practicing with field artillery the war came to an end. He sailed, nonetheless, for South Africa and was mortified to find that he was the only soldier on the troopship who had not been decorated. "I thought the only answer was to commit suicide. Well, after some thought I decided against suicide. Instead I continued on to my battery in South Africa where, as fate would have it, I suffered a bad steeplechase accident. I was put on half-pay and sent back to England to recover. While I was home I asked a friend of mine — mind you, it was a pretty risky thing being a friend of mine in those days — for a job. He sent me around to the War Office where a gentleman behind a huge desk asked me if I wanted to go to Northern Rhodesia. 'I would love to,' I replied. 'Where is it?' "

Sir Stewart thereupon spent three years on a boundary commission in Northern Rhodesia. He was the only one of the six men who learned to speak Chibemba, the native dialect, and whether as a result or not, the only one of the group to survive the trip.

Throughout my life in Africa I have experienced the greatest help and friendliness from the African people, and I cannot recollect an occasion when they failed to help me when I needed it.
— Sir Michael Blundell,
So Rough a Wind

"During my first few months on the commission I did not at all like the country; shooting was my only form of entertainment." But after a while the primitiveness of Northern Rhodesia began to charm him and it was not long, he asserts, before he had fallen in love with both the country and the Bemba people. When he returned to England he submitted a request to the British South Africa Company to settle in Northern Rhodesia. The head of the

company told Sir Stewart's aunt that he would grant her
nephew twenty-five thousand acres at ten shillings an acre
on the one condition that she did not go there herself.

After the war Sir Stewart returned and in 1928 with his
uncle's financing he began to build the house. During the
four years it took to complete it an enormous amount of
labor was required. "I got tremendous satisfaction," he
said, "from the thought that I was building an empire in a
land where people were happy together."

"Developing a cash crop was the great problem. Since
we were so isolated we needed to grow something which
was neither heavy nor bulky." Upon a suggestion of his
uncle's, Sir Stewart decided to produce essential oils from
fruit. From ten thousand acres of trees they extracted one
million gallons of juice, which was finally reduced to
twenty-five gallons of essential oil. Their final product was
sold as a scent retainer to soap manufacturers in Europe.
From this harvest alone Shiwa Ngandu generated an annual profit of six thousand pounds. The boom lasted for
almost two decades until suddenly in 1947 the trees were
devastated by a crippling virus, and within several years
there was nothing left of the lime trees. "If I had been
younger," Sir Stewart said, "I would have begun all over
again, but, as it was, it seemed to be too much of an agony.
The Lord, as you know, hates primary producers."

"That is the beginning and I can't tell you the end.
What do you think is going to happen to us, Henry?"
Henry did not know. He shrugged his shoulders and
smiled. ("You know, Henry is, as my grandmother used
to say, very well connected. He's the grandson of Chitama-
kula, the famous Bemba chief.")

"I have every hope for this place in the future. My

daughter and her children fit in very well with life here. While I'm alive I've found that the best way to live with one's children is by keeping them as far away as possible. They have one corner of the house and I have mine. We rarely see each other except at teatime. When I die I think this place will continue to prosper, perhaps in a different way. Who knows?"

We had luncheon with Sir Stewart in his private dining room, which was decorated in Gustave Doré prints. Hartebeest croquettes were served on a silver platter and the beer came in glass-bottomed tankards. When we had finished the coffee he showed us the chapel, an airy Spanish-style building with long wooden benches where his retainers sat. On the wall was a plaque commemorating his aunt and uncle for their generosity in helping him build Shiwa Ngandu.

At Shiwa there is plenty of time to reflect and to wonder. Memories, half-thoughts, long-forgotten lessons float through the corridors and along the footpaths of the estate with a mournful transience. It seems as though they are willed upon Shiwa Ngandu, just as it was willed upon the countryside, by the whimsy of its creator. Over the doorway leading into the house is the inscription *Servez raison*, an incongruous suggestion in this huge feudal estate set in the wilds of Africa. Shiwa Ngandu does not belong to this world of reason and purpose, of geometry and dirty hands; nor does it belong to Africa. The thorns and dust beyond the eucalyptus trees and beyond the brick gates spread far into the distance, almost invisible to the naked eye. It is as though the house was built to re-create another world and has, with the passage of time, outgrown its original model.

It seems to be a mistake of nature that Sir Stewart's face is severe. Old age has gouged it with deep, hard lines and has given it an almost demonic resolution. Only when he speaks does it mellow. The soft creaking sounds of his voice seem to smooth out the lines, forcing his eyes and mouth into a smile. "One doth not know," he once quoted, "how much an ill word may empoison liking."

Shiwa Ngandu seems to have outlasted the principles which were ascribed to it. When it was first constructed Sir Stewart entertained the hope that it would contribute to some new order of empire. But the vagaries of nature and the limitations of his ambition reduced it from a vision to a dream. Once, Shiwa Ngandu represented the antique principle of lordship invested in one man through property and maintained through his benevolence. Today it merely stands for his ability to exploit the "winds of change." Its real test of longevity is still to come. Already the old hopes and visions are beginning to be replaced by the new, seemingly transient, principles of Africa. Walls are crumbling, flower beds are overgrown and the bell at the foot of the garden no longer rings out the hours. Sir Stewart senses that what he once began will end with his life. The uniqueness of his creation will be forfeited to something less personal, and a new generation not so inclined to such ambitious and lonely hopes will convert Shiwa to its own ends.

They tell the Tale of Empire, do these winds; wild calling to wild, and the urge and surge of blood which must carry out people willy nilly into the last attainable confines of a finite earth, there to persist, absorb, dictate, boss, and impose our Will.

— Ewart S. Grogan,
Introduction to
Farming and Planning
in British East Africa,
1917

CHAPTER IV

Perhaps on some quiet night the tremor of far-off drums, sinking, swelling, a tremor vast, faint; a sound weird, appealing, suggestive, and wild — and perhaps with as profound a meaning as the sound of bells in a Christian country.

— Joseph Conrad, *Heart of Darkness*

Many years ago in a remote valley of Africa four White Fathers were enjoying the last of the day's heat on the veranda of their mission house. They had loosened their collars since the weather was heavy with the expectancy of the rains. Unbeknown to them, a leopard had sprung through an open window at the back of the house and was stealthily making its way toward the veranda. When it reached the front door the Father Superior was the first to notice it. Without hesitating a second he rose to his feet, took several imperious steps toward the animal and rapped his hands together as though to teach it manners. "Be off," he said. The leopard turned and fled through the house into the bush.

Not far from this valley, but many years later, the spirit of nationalism spread through the villages like a sea of lava. For many months every white man, regardless of who he was, came to symbolize the cause of hunger and privation. Rocks were thrown at cars, houses were set alight, one white man was killed and a District Commissioner was wounded. Finally, anticipating the situation would deteriorate, the colonial government sent an airplane from the capital to appraise the conditions of the few scattered white people in the interior of the country. The pilot was instructed to give particular attention to a mission station which was run by twelve white families and whose proximity to the riot-torn area concerned the Governor. The pilot circled the red-brick mission houses and was hesitating whether to turn back when he saw written on the ground in whitewashed stones: "Ephesians 2–14." He made a mental note of it and once he had arrived at the capital he located the passage in the Bible and found that it meant: "He is our bond of peace; He has made the two nations one, breaking down the wall that was a barrier to us, in His own mortal nature."

Missionaries were among the first to instruct the worlds of Europe and America of the hazards which faced life on the African continent. They were in the advance guard of white men to take up residence in the jungles, bush and deserts where life was uncomfortable and death, which they accepted as part of their mission, was generally cruel. For them, propagating Christianity was only part of their task; staying alive was as important. The high rate of mortality among missionaries in Africa attested to the fact that death might easily overtake them before their personal objectives had been realized. It was therefore of the utmost importance for them to devote a good part of the day to the job of avoiding or reducing risks. The extremes of life in Africa rarely allowed a man a second chance. At the Holy Ghost Mission outside of Bagamoyo on the Indian Ocean there is a large graveyard which documents the price Christianity had to pay in Africa. Well over fifty percent of the graves are those of missionaries who died before the age of thirty, several as young as twenty-four. Few lived beyond the age of forty (those who did seemed to survive to ripe old ages). And it is ironic that in spite of all these sacrifices the Mission of the White Fathers, founded in 1873 and today staffed by eleven men, has converted only seven hundred men out of a total population of nine thousand.

In the course of this struggle for survival missionaries tended to grow into a different breed from their colleagues who stayed at home. To struggle is, in part, to suffer and to change. Missionaries came to Africa to upset an order and, in turn, they discovered that they became a part of it.

Africa is a self-conscious land; it is spoken of with human characteristics for it affects people as if it had a character and a soul. While no person could contain all of its conflicting temperaments, its overall fickleness resembles that of man. Africa comprises a sampling of most of the world's store of what is organic and inorganic, human and animal, all of which conspires to engrave a mark on those who give of themselves to it. The lessons are thus two-way.

Missionaries, by the nature of their jobs, learn to accept the pleasures and pains of life with fatalistic steadiness. Their visions are generally tempered with realism for they learn that progress should only be measured by its reverses and that one advance may be followed by two setbacks. And it is inevitable that they develop a sense of humor. The common denominator of African behavior is as it was in the time of David Livingstone, basically un-Christian, for witch doctors, polygamy and ritualism still persist in addition to the ever-increasing number of problems stimulated by societies on the move.

Missionaries belong to a strong breed, for they must, in spite of their mission, preserve their own identities in a world distinctly different from the one in which they were born. Every day they are tortured by a new Africa, and every day they must learn to accept it and reject it according to their basic human instincts. Strength is required to preserve one's judgment after years of malaria, heat and exhaustion. In addition to those traits of character required by their church they must possess qualities which mark them as achievers in a primitive, secular world, such as leadership, endurance and guts, for their converts judge them not only on the basis of faith but also in terms of how they qualify as men. The missionary who learns to feel at home in Africa is hence a realist, since he must learn to accept his own humanity. Africa can teach a white man about himself. To be a success helping others one must accept a biological responsibility to oneself and one's own race. One cannot *escape* to Africa in order to do good, for it contains the spectrum of humanity and to go there is but an immersion into oneself.

The great concentrations of mission stations are along the old slave routes. Lake Nyasa (or Malawi), for instance, was almost entirely encircled by churches in an attempt to restore its people to an earlier status quo after the bloodshed of the slave trade. At the Church of Scotland Mission on the western shore the missionaries can train their telescopes to the east and see, towering above the Livingstone Mountains, the spire of a Roman Catholic cathedral. Until recently there was a fierce competition between mission stations for converts; today it seems to have almost disappeared. One missionary explained to me that all Christian religions in Africa, regardless of dogmatic differences, must accept the same peculiarly African obstacles to conversion. The Church of Scotland, for instance, once preached total abstinence in spite of the African love for drinking beer. Today it has retreated on this matter although most of the missionaries themselves are still teetotalers. It is gradually being recognized that to be effective the church must make certain concessions and compromises for the benefit of the African. Christianity, according to a younger generation of missionaries, should be molded to the African temperament and allowed, at the risk of losing its Western biases and traditions, to become a part of the black man's heritage. The missionary's place in Africa is therefore an uncomfortable one, for he must learn to yield his position and sometimes his person to a different culture.

Is a missionary most successful when he identifies with the African mentality or when he stubbornly maintains his personal differences? Obviously, there is no absolute answer, but I am strongly convinced that to relinquish one's background in order to be more effective with people of another background is both vain and deceptive. Do what he may, the white man is known as the *bwana* by the African; his white skin has come to symbolize an apartness, a difference in outlook. *Bwana* has also come to signify "master," and regardless of the disrepute into which the white skin has at times fallen, the word seems to retain this meaning. For this reason the missionary invariably finds himself placed in the category of the leader — a position which he can use to his advantage by allowing it to enhance his spiritual influence and color his role with an attractive uncommonness.

From Livingstonia Mission there is a hazy view of Lake Nyasa, a now forgotten highway of the slave trade. The

The natives of Africa I had not met before; all the same they came into my life as a kind of answer to some call in my own nature to dreams of childhood perhaps, or to poetry read and cherished long ago, or to emotions and instincts deep down in the mind.
— Isak Dinesen, On Mottoes of My Life

green, airy country has made the red-brick, factory-like
buildings with their corrugated tin roofs seem misfits.
Even the church was built along austere lines. Above its
doors there is a stained-glass window depicting a stern
David Livingstone surrounded by primly clothed Africans. The mission was established just a few years after
his death, and in the first five years of its existence it lost
three missionaries to tropical diseases and gained only one
convert. Today malaria, blackwater and bilharzia are all
relics of the past, since after several relocations the mission's site is now high above the disease line. The missionaries are primarily young men. They have brought
their families to live with them in Africa and they stay at
the mission for a term of five years before returning to
Scotland.

George Campbell was our host, and after his wife had
treated us to a cake which had been prepared for the visit
of the British High Commissioner that morning, we wandered together along the dirt roads of the mission. Occasionally Campbell waved to one of his students, but once
he had begun to talk to me his eyes seemed no longer to
focus on physical things. Soon we found ourselves in the
church, and sitting down in one of the rough-hewn pews,
he explained to me that he had left school at the age of
fourteen for financial reasons and had spent the next
eleven years of his life as a postal clerk. He admitted that
he had always been inclined toward a religious life, but at
the age of nineteen he suddenly decided to play a more active part in it. "It was something that grew on me. I was
too lazy to study very hard so I took a modified course lasting five years. I can't say I had any blinding light — that
would have been too handy. I said to God, 'I think you

want me to go into the ministry, but if you don't you'd
better tell me fast.' Well, I didn't get a reply in the nega-
tive so I kept on. Then, in 1958 when I had completed my
seminary work, my wife and I looked around to see what
place needed us. We decided that since Central Africa was
going through economic, social and political changes it
would need religious strength. It seemed that in this part
of the world we could make the greatest possible contribu-
tion, so we came and have been here ever since. My work is
primarily religious, but I believe that a man who is helped
religiously is also helped socially. A good Christian is a
good citizen. This is God's world and therefore you take
care of it better if you plant a garden and don't beat your
wife."

When the country was in the hands of the British the
Church of Scotland waged an unending battle in defense
of the political rights of the Africans. It did so because it
believed the government was not consulting with the people of the country. During the latter part of the struggle
for independence, when other missions were arguing that
they did not need to pander friendship with Africans
through politics, the Church of Scotland Mission assumed
such an intense role in defense of the Africans' political
rights that it was accused of disloyalty to its own nation.
George Campbell explained his church's stand by saying
that in Scotland the Presbyterians have traditionally over-
looked the division between church and state. There, syn-
ods are divided into parishes and the minister of each parish looks after all the members of his parish regardless of
their religion. "It's the same here in Central Africa,"
Campbell said. "We believe there is a certain totality in
life. We must help our people not only religiously but also

in matters which are going to better the individual's life on earth."

Campbell had been born into a poor family in Edinburgh, and almost from the very beginning he found himself struggling for survival. In many ways the class to which he had then belonged resembled the one which he was now helping. Just as he might once have defended himself against an exploiting bourgeoisie in Scotland, so had he agitated against such a class in Africa. Once he would have undertaken to fight for social rights; today he had found that quiet persistence was just as effective.

In a more subtle way Campbell struggled to preserve his own identity. On the one hand, he was anxious to point out the similarities between his own temperament and that of the African, and on the other, he felt no inclination to bridge their differences. He did not consider the African tradition a just cause for rearranging either Christianity or himself. Since monogamy, European clothes, a six-day week and a frugal life were good enough for him they were also good enough for the African. Although in church he sang the hymns in Chitambuko, the local dialect, and after the service he introduced me with pride to his old parishioners dressed in topis from the days of David Livingstone, Campbell conducted his life as he would have in Scotland. He was determined to impart the Christian ideals to Africa and if, in so doing, he also subjected them to his own secular ideals, so much the better. In Africa there is little sense in making apologies.

The Roman Catholic Mission in Karonga was not as austere. The three White Fathers lived in a long refectory building, which although certainly not luxurious made little pretense at asceticism. Imported sauces and wines covered their dining-room table, and in the corner of their sitting room there was a large stack of cigarettes. Father Chiasson, who had met me at the door, explained, "None of us have taken a vow of poverty; consequently we are allowed to live off the vast sum of four and six [sixty-three cents] per day. We make ends meet by eliciting contributions from friends at home."

We sat with him around a table in a room whose walls were covered with books. He removed his sunglasses to reveal two clean spots on the sides of his dust-covered nose. His white Edwardian beard had turned red with the dust and his balding head was streaked with sweat. He explained to us that although his name was French he had been born in Boston. Like one of his sisters, he had chosen a religious life at a young age, and after studying philosophy for two years at Laval University, he decided the time was ripe for entering the order. His explanation for joining the White Fathers was typically irreverent: he hated to shave and the White Fathers was one of the few religious orders that encouraged beards. As a boy of twenty, his prime concern was for excitement. "I wanted to go to the Sahara and lead an adventurous life," he explained.

The White Fathers had been formed in 1868 for the purpose of presenting the Arabs with an alternative to Islam. The Fathers adopted the Arab dress, the long, flowing jellaba and the beaded fez, and spent several years learning Arabic in order to be able to infiltrate the people. But the resistance to an outside religion was far stronger than had been expected, and even today, after almost a century of missionary activity, there are few converts in North Africa. Father Chiasson's training consisted of five years

*The more we received
a modern education the
more spiritually illiter-
ate we were becoming.
. . . We might know
some physics or as-
tronomy, but we did
not notice if the moon
waxed or waned, and
we were losing wonder
at the visage of the
stars.*

— *Gerard Wallop,
Earl of Portsmouth,*
A Knot of Roots

in a seminary followed by three at a mission near Tunis and one in Algiers. His dreams of adventure in the Sahara rapidly dissolved when he was sent to Central Africa, which he has found to be just as exciting as the fabled desert. Apart from the satisfaction he derives from his work, there is no other place in which he would rather live. "You can have the States," he told me. "There is too much tension and pressure there. I once saw a boy of fifteen dying in Bellevue of heart disease. Do you think that could have happened to him in Africa? We work hard here, but there is no pressure. During the rainy season we might have to bicycle through deep mud for twenty-five miles, but it's all fun. Nothing is humdrum, and that's what's exciting. Africa is not geared to seconds, minutes and hours but to years and sometimes decades. That allows us to devote more time to the major matters of life, not the petty boring ones."

During the thirty years that Father Chiasson has been in Africa, he has returned home only twice. It is the duty of every White Father to raise money for the mission while on leave at home. He spent his entire time driving from one church to another. In one Sunday at a wealthy Chicago church he raised thirteen hundred dollars. For him there was little satisfaction in such work. His last leave at home was for three years: far too long a period, he complained. His first tour of duty in Africa had been for eleven years, his second for thirteen, his third: "Who knows?" he said. "I hope at least fifteen. I trust that when I die I shall do so here on African soil, preferably in my boots."

At the time of his profession, Father Chiasson vowed to devote his life to the people of Africa. During the Second World War it was therefore impossible for him to serve in

the American forces. Instead, he joined the King's African
Rifles as Chaplain and served the war effort in Ceylon,
Burma and India. At the end of the war he lost his American citizenship because he had fought in a foreign army,
and only after a long struggle, and with the help of influ-
ential members of the Church, was it restored to him. Father Chiasson recalls his army career with nostalgia because it was there he learned how to shoot. His instructor
was an Australian who had once been a bodyguard for Al
Capone. "He used to ask me about the striptease clubs
in Boston until he discovered I was a chaplain." Father
Chiasson learned to shoot every sort of gun — a talent
which had served him well as a missionary. His parishioners are continually asking him to protect them from dangerous animals. "I don't hunt that much nowadays," he
admits. "The Canadian White Fathers are the ones who
do all the hunting and poaching."

Just then one of the Canadians in question, Father
Crousset, came in and, sitting down, silently drew on a
cigarette. He had been up in the hills and his tunic was
covered with fine red dust. At Father Chiasson's remark
his face slowly broadened into a smile, and he explained to
me that because there was little game in this region the
enforcement of conservation laws was casual. Since hunting is respected as a great talent by Africans he felt that he
was adding to the Church's prestige by poaching. "I am
rationalizing," he admitted. "I just love to hunt." Father
Stumpf, a German, broke in at this point in the conversation and pointed out that the White Fathers' Mission,
thanks to its prestige, had indeed affected the community.
"I know," he affirmed, "that Christianity has helped these
people. Go to the jail, for example, and you will see that

only ten percent of the prisoners are Christians, compared to a much higher percentage of Christians in the community at large."

I returned early in the morning of the next day and walked around the grounds of the mission with the three Fathers. Standing in front of the school were two Africans dressed in Western clothes, self-consciously smoking cigarettes. The sight was offensive to the three missionaries. "Look at this," Father Chiasson said. "Africa's greatest problem staring us in the face: give a native a primary school education, a pair of long trousers, a hat, a tie and a cigarette. No white man would dare wear that getup in this climate and yet these characters consider themselves civilized in it. It seems they've learned all the wrong things." Sin, according to the Fathers, was closely allied to the veneer of civilization. They saw themselves surrounded by an ever-increasing number of hybrid Westerners, of Africans who have chosen to escape from the suffocation of the eventless life of the *shamba* and the village by identifying with an unfamiliar, often hostile culture. Rebellion, the Fathers believed, was unrewarding in Africa. The missionaries felt uneasy that the new Africa was replacing the euphoric languor of tribal life with the hectic pace of the West. To them the only advancement that really mattered was that of the soul. Progress must only be calculated by spiritual well-being. Although both they and the missionaries from the Church of Scotland deplored nakedness, the White Fathers were not committed to substituting Western dress for the traditional African one. The local cloth was sufficient. Furthermore, education by itself, they felt, was useless, but when it was given a religious bias, it served a valuable purpose. The White Fathers, being of different nationalities, were not interested in propagating the values of a culture alongside religion. They were of one purpose as missionaries, for religion was essentially all they had in common.

The White Fathers viewed the black world which surrounded them not with the all-encompassing interest which motivated the missionaries from the Church of Scotland, but rather with a decided arbitrariness. Only when a man had emerged into the world of Christianity was he to be accepted as an individual; otherwise he was a blank, an integer in a numberless world. Conversion was like a sudden acquisition of personality, a giant step toward becoming a person with a name and a character.

The White Fathers in Karonga seemed to be of an old school; their beards and their long white tunics gave them a distinctive bearing. They were like magicians to a people who believe in magic; their distinctiveness was their talent, and it had little to do with class or privilege. They belonged to that breed of men who flourish when apart from like men, for Christianity was more meaningful to them when it was surrounded by paganism. When we left them, enclosed by a sea of very black faces, it appeared for a brief moment that theirs was a lonely life. But before they were lost in the dust of our car I saw, in the rearview mirror, the three White Fathers waving their arms. Their white tunics, caught by the rising heat, spread, as in a mirage, through all the crowd.

For almost a week thereafter we traveled through missionary country. The signs of Baptist, Episcopalian, Seventh Day Adventist and Roman Catholic missions hung along every portion of our route. There was Father Tom from a Maryknoll mission, who talked about the world series; Father Mike, who took us swimming in a crater lake near an old German fort on the southern border of Tanzania; Sister Pauline, a doctor who was waging a single-handed war against malaria, syphilis and elephantiasis on the eastern shore of Lake Nyasa; and Brother Bertram, who belonged to a monastic order which seemed to have been modeled by Rabelais. Once when we stopped in a patch of broken shade for lunch near the Ruvuma River, a motorcyclist drove past us cheerfully waving his hand. We heard the sound of the engine fade away into the distance and then it slowed down and returned toward us. Soon the motorcycle came into sight again. When the wavy-haired driver propped the machine up onto its stand he explained to us that it had suddenly occurred to him after he had passed us that we might have broken down. We offered him some pineapple slices and when he had gulped them down he introduced himself as Father Joseph of Nandembo Mission. He was touring his parish and was displeased with the activities of his flock. "Ah, it's a losing battle around here," he said, with an unmistakable Dublin accent. "I have to go all over the country to deal penance to these blooming Christians. Not a one of them seems to be behaving himself. There's only one thing I can say for sure, the Muslims make better citizens than do these Christians." He explained to us that since the Muslims have more than one wife they plow bigger and better fields than do the Christians, and consequently they have less time for "mischief." Father Joseph also pointed out that the Muslim, unlike the Christian, is terrified of the witch doctor's medicine, and as a result he is more reluctant to violate the tribal code. The witch doctor oversees a highly

ritualized system of punishments and rewards, but those
who do not believe in him need have no fear of his penal-
ties. "Ah," Father Joseph sighed. "What's more important
than making them Christians is making them civilized.
It's all a man can do from going round the bend out here. I
read a book now and then to keep my feet on the ground.
There's nothing like a decadent novel to sort a man out.
Take for instance Kathleen Winsor's *Forever Amber*.
Now there's a story. Well, I won't bore you with my pecca-
dilloes. Look, stop at my house in Tunduru for a beer and
when you get to Masasi stay at the Catholic Mission there.
Don't worry, the priests won't talk religion." He started
the motorcycle and, waving to us, he yelled, "Just say the
mad Irishman sent you. They'll know who you mean." Before we had a chance to wave good-bye he had fishtailed
around a corner and was out of sight.

The next morning, after staying the night at the Catholic Mission in Masasi, we did an about-face and had tea
with the Anglicans. Trevor Huddleston, the Bishop of
Masasi, met us at the door of his thatch-roofed house.
From the manner in which he spoke he could easily have
been an Oxford don: he spoke in an imperturbable and
deliberate voice, as though he arrived at the answer to even
the simplest question by scrutinizing self-examination. Yet
I gradually began to realize that there was another side to
his nature that was singularly anti-intellectual: he was
irrepressibly in love with Africa. When I later read his
book *Naught for Your Comfort*, it was evident that he did
not romanticize about the land. "No natural beauty," he
wrote, "could ever so lay hold on my heart as to make me
weep for leaving it. Others may be created differently; I
have never been able to feel that nostalgia for places, how-

ever lovely. And, after all, Africa is a cruel place rather than a beautiful one." He had been touched by the human side of Africa, by the dark faces huddled around coal braziers, by the endless padding of flat feet along the roadsides. What is more, Africa had accepted him. Little boys and girls huddled in the folds of his tunic, laughed when he laughed and followed him with their eyes. He was one of those strangely gifted people who, while retaining their identities, have acquired an intuitive response to the African.

Above his desk was a painting of an old prune-faced woman pounding mealies. Under it, written in schoolboy letters, was the inscription "Mother of Africa." He leaned back in his chair and gazed at the *makuti* beans. His long plastic face was relaxed. His eyes never left me. "It's a matter of whether Africa wants me, not whether I want Africa," he explained. "There's no reason why one should force oneself on Africa. I think anyone who is going to do a job has to identify with the place. Since a priest is with people, your whole work depends on the relation you have with your people. I can assure you that there are thousands of white men who have left Africa because they cannot identify with the people. The place is either too big or too savage. There are other people who tried too hard and became too affected by it. For them Africa also grew to be savage. You see, you must be detached."

Bishop Huddleston has spent almost all his working life in Africa. In 1943 he was appointed to the Anglican Mission in Sophiatown, an African suburb of sprawling Johannesburg, and for thirteen years he devoted himself to the problems of the urbanized African. Finally, on the verge of being arrested by the government, he was recalled to England. There he worked for four years until in September 1960 he took up the post of Bishop of Masasi. In many ways it is for him a more difficult job than working in the slums of Johannesburg, for in South Africa he was dealing with the working class: men and women who were at least peripherally sophisticated in the ways of the West. In southern Tanzania, on the other hand, ninety percent of the people are not earning a living. Their only occupation is to scratch their meager subsistence from the ground. Bishop Huddleston admitted that he found it far more difficult a task to communicate with such people. They were, after all, peasant farmers and he was an educated Westerner. Even members of the Peace Corps, who he felt were very sympathetic, were not able to eliminate their prejudices within a two-year period.

He was brave enough to admit that he had not found all the answers. The world could not simply be made one with love alone. Something beyond tolerance was required. He admitted that every day he had to renew his struggle and resolve his problems. On the one hand he could not help but become involved with his people, and on the other, he realized that if he were to succeed his personality must become an abstraction to them. Since he was certain that he was to be the last English Bishop of Masasi, it was of utmost importance for him to separate the "Englishness" from the governorship of the diocese and, in turn, to strip away from the faith the Western forms which had accumulated around it. The problem for him was to distinguish accretions from substance. Eventually, he explained, missionaries should all be Africans, since a European, he believed, can only imperfectly guide a black man in matters of the soul. Bishop Huddleston explained that the African has an

But in my heart is the true aristocratic claim to be putting more into African life than I take from it. If I can help the economy well and good; if however humbly I can help the long safari of the mind across a thousand years of bitter experience in a generation, well and better.

— *Gerard Wallop,*
Earl of Portsmouth,
A Knot of Roots

innate sense of expression. "Just this morning," he said, "there was a wedding, and outside of the church drums were beating. Why not bring them inside? Surely the Church can accommodate non-Western sacred music." One breakthrough was the practice of circumcision, which he had allowed to become a part of the process of Christian initiation. He hopes that in the future the major changes will not come from liberal European thought but rather from within, from the Africans themselves.

Our tea had gone cold. Bishop Huddleston's cup, balanced on his knee, was rattling on its saucer and now that he had answered my questions he drank the tea enthusiastically. When the cup was empty he sat back in his chair and, like a pool filling with water, his face assumed a comfortable glow. He was at home under the thatch, and the sleepy sound of voices on the stoep was a part of his element. Outside, the sun was high, diffused in a moisture-laden sky. The rains had still not come and it was hot.

When we left Masasi we did not expect to see the Bishop again, but in the late afternoon, on our way to the sea, our paths crossed once more. Just before sunset he walked into the home of Ionides, with whom we had spent the afternoon. I was surprised to note that the Bishop was a friend of Ionides, for at first I could think of nothing the two men had in common. Ionides, an Englishman of distant Greek parentage, is a dried specimen of the bush. He has a hollowed-out face which supports an erratic moustache and an unkempt patch of white hair. His background is, by all standards, unorthodox. After a tour of duty in the Indian Army and the King's African Rifles which succeeded his dismissal from Rugby, he took to poaching. This profession was soon superseded by a ca-

reer in the Game Department, which led to his present vo-
cation as a snake-catcher. Today, in his seventies, Ionides
has few regrets. Old age changed him from an adventurer
into a scientist, and all that matters to him now is accuracy
and the tangible truth. He considers himself the supremely
independent man. His usual dress is a shredded brown
sweater, khaki pants and snake boots. He owns neither ties
nor socks, refused to lime-wash his kitchen, as is the custom
in Africa, and flagrantly disregards politics in his dealings
with the local people. Facts and achievements are all that
matter to him. His gods are the king cobras, the Caesars
and the achievers of history.

We had been talking of Genghis Khan when Bishop
Huddleston walked into the snake-filled room. Momentarily Ionides squinted his eyes to see who it was, and then
his normally impassive face broke into a smile. It was clear
that the two men were old friends. "What will you have?"
Ionides asked.

"Brandy and water, please," came the answer.

"Allow me," Ionides said, full of magnanimity, "to
press my electric buzzer for the servant." Not knowing
what to expect we looked at Ionides, who drew a mouthful
of air into his lungs and in a military voice bellowed for
the boy.

Trevor Huddleston loosened his collar and tipped his
chair onto its back legs. His day had been hot, full of dusty
work, but now, finally, there was a chance to relax. The
two men did not talk of religion. Bishop Huddleston
wanted to find out about snakes, so the conversation
lingered over Gabon vipers, Egyptian cobras and the sixty-
four green mambas in the next room. Ionides then mentioned, for a reason best known to him, that he had once

eaten monitor lizard. Soon the discussion began to range over a myriad of subjects.

When I left it was late. I looked down from the veranda to the blackness below in which somewhere the Ruvuma flowed. It was one of Ionides's greatest delights to know that there was not one light visible. He called it "darkest Africa." Inside the house I could hear the two men laughing and soon Ionides's "electric buzzer" sounded for the second time. With the soft scuffle of his bare feet treading on the gravel the "boy" appeared from the darkness and stood outside the screen door awaiting his orders.

The two men inside the room were old friends. Obviously it was not part of the missionary's job to have a brandy with a snake-catcher, but neither was chasing leopards off his veranda nor quoting the Bible in whitewashed stones.

CHAPTER V

You have tremendous views as you get up above the African highlands, surprising combinations and changes of light and colouring, the rainbow on the green sunlit land, the gigantic upright clouds and big wild black storms, all swing round you in a race and a dance. The lashing hard showers of rain whiten the air askance. The language is short of words for the experiences of flying, and will have to invent new words with time. When you have flown over the Rift Valley and the volcanoes of Suswa and Longonot, you have travelled far and have been to the lands on the other side of the moon. You may at other times fly low enough to see the animals on the plains and to feel towards them as God did when he had just created them, and before he had commissioned Adam to give them names.

— Isak Dinesen, *Out of Africa*

In THE morning we flew, much as Isak Dinesen once had. I thought I saw the bare ridges of the Ngong Hills in the far distance where once she and Denys Finch-Hatton had postponed tea to watch a herd of buffalo; later we soared beside an eagle, stopping the engine to hear it make its wild bitter cry. We saw the clouds of November wiping the pasty face of the Rift Valley in the early morning and the escarpment to the east rising above us through the haze. The thermals lifted the fragile plane into the thin air until a sudden storm bore down upon us and carried us off to Lake Hannington from where, with the rain exploding on the windscreen, we scampered a few hundred feet above the floor of the Rift to the sanctuary of a farmer's field.

For a fleeting second in the air I had seen all of Africa, a catchment of paradoxes, a victim of other worlds. When I drove away from the field I was anxious to see more, to ask questions about the men who plowed the furrows and discovered the land. I was to meet Sir Michael Blundell at his farm southeast of Nakuru, for I had been told that if anyone could talk about the white men of Kenya it was he. I stopped once to ask directions at an Indian *duka*, full of rolls of colored cloth and the musty smell of a patient clientele, and heard the weather report interspersed with thunderclaps of static. The rains had only just reached the coast, leaving the highlands in a state of expectancy. Every day when the heat reached its peak, thunderheads would build up in the sky and for a fleeting second rain would clear the air — just enough to make the grass glisten but not enough to change it into a deep-green lushness.

Sir Michael met me on his veranda and in silent judgment walked me into his sitting room. He introduced me to his wife and the two of them sat next to each other on a sofa. He was a powerful man with a florid complexion, yet when he spoke he intoned his words with gentle precision. By experience he was a farmer — rejoicing with deep yeoman satisfaction in a straight furrow, willing to take chances with new crops and glad to know that the land as far as the hills was his own. For many years this farm had been his retreat from the battlefield of politics. It was once his escape, now his home. He was sensitive by nature, too proud to admit that his temperament might not be suited to harsh criticism and backroom judgments, yet too full of convictions to allow a misguided history to assert itself.

There were few introductory remarks. Almost from the very beginning he submerged me in his farseeing views. It was as though I was once again in the airplane looking down across the dry land which swept from Menengai to Ol Bolossat. "Africa," he said, "was never a white man's country. It might have been, but he chose to colonize it in a period when he was not ruthless enough to exterminate the indigenous people. A hundred years before he came here,

Every morning now it took the heavy, wooled sky an hour or so longer to clear and you could feel the rains coming, as they moved steadily north, as surely as though you watched them on a chart.

— Ernest Hemingway,
The Green Hills
of Africa

you were destroying your Indians in America. I guess the white man was just a bit too late in arriving in Africa. His greatest mistake was supposing that despite the indigenous peoples this could be a white man's country. For many years, in fact, it looked as though it might be just that, but in recent times to consider Kenya a white man's country was to overlook the obvious fact that the white man is greatly outnumbered by the black man. Facts, sadly enough, are what count." He paused briefly to let me mull over his words and then he continued. "I have found however that although the white man has no claim to the destiny of Kenya, he still has a place in this country. He is here to advise and help and I think that from now on he will be welcomed by the Africans. Whatever animosity there is today will be gone in the next generation. I for one surely do not regret having stayed on."

He settled back into the sofa and looked out at his land varnished by the evening sunlight. He began to tell me how it was before, about those who came for a lifetime yet left after only a few years, and of the others who were not disillusioned by black nationalism and remain on the land today. The railway, which reached Victoria Nyanza in 1901, initiated white settlement. First came the pure pioneers. They were least of all businessmen or colonizers. To them the adventure of Africa was the challenge of a new life in an unspoiled country and the freedom of living in what virtually amounted to a no-man's-land. Few if any of these men still live today. There was a second category consisting of those who applied their adventuresome spirit to creating a product out of an undeveloped land. This was the average pioneer — a man who was engaged in making things like crops, breeds of animals and houses, and who in the beginning was not necessarily interested in the human aspect of his job. "Look at me," Sir Michael remarked. "Last year when I was fifty-eight years old I planted tea knowing full well that I would not see any economic return for five years. What a crack idea, and yet, I suppose it and a lot of other crack ideas are what made Kenya a rather special farming community." The third category of settlers, Sir Michael continued, consisted of many of those who arrived late in the making of the country. It was their intention to live as they had lived before, with all the conveniences and comforts of a modern country. According to Sir Michael they never ceased looking over their shoulders to make sure "the unknown" was not about to stab them in the back.

But the fact remains that if a native is told to do anything, and it is within the bounds of his diabolical ingenuity to do it wrong, he will do it wrong; and if he cannot do it wrong, he will not do it right.

— Ewart S. Grogan and Arthur Sharp, From the Cape to Cairo

Sir Michael maintained that with change has come the real test of the pioneer. He and many others have managed to adjust to the new Kenya and the sometimes uncomfortable balance of power. Those who sought a sanctuary because they could not adjust to life in England discovered that it was equally hard to adjust to life in Kenya. Most of these, he went on to say, rushed down to Rhodesia and South Africa as soon as Kenya became independent.

A heavy cloud bank had built up along the horizon and was making the distant reaches of the Rift look tarnished and ripe. Somewhere to the east was Mount Kenya, glistening in another world above the haze, and beyond it the Northern Frontier District, a wrinkled slag heap of volcanic rubble and desert. It was here in 1898 that John Boyes, a fierce Yorkshireman, established himself as king of the Kikuyu, since he was the first white man that tribe had seen. When he died in 1951 Kenya had run the cycle of white settlement and was unconsciously approaching a new age. The view from Sir Michael Blundell's farm added little to what Boyes had witnessed in his lifetime save that I could see miles of country still innocent of progress. The view, I thought at the time, was a tribute to the wildness of Africa, for in spite of roads, telephone wires and cement factories the bush had still not been entirely conquered. At this, my last stop in Kenya, I felt that I had completed a long safari through that country's past and that Sir Michael, paradoxically, was symbolic of both its white history and of change, since he eulogized the convictions of the pioneer, welcomed their end and heralded a new age, defiant of the one which had come before.

Since it appeared that conviction, disillusionment and change were fellow travelers in white man's Africa, my safari through Kenya might have begun anywhere: perhaps with Pat Hemingway, Ernest's son, surveying his sixteen years on the African continent and saying that he did not think "Africa had lived up to its expectations"; or the sight of Giriama tribesmen water-skiing at the exclusive Mnarani Club on the coast; or watching more elephants than I could count leave the Athi River and ponderously climb up onto the Yatta Plateau at the first sign of rain. In Africa the primeval seemed to mix in an uneasy alliance with the synthetic. The frontier had vanished leaving maudlin reminders of an age in which half-measures were never tolerated but which seemed to coexist among the new vistas of a hybrid life. I looked into the past and saw the long lines of safaris weaving snakelike across unfenced country and wondered whether they might add a sense of uncommonness to the future.

Mary Anne and I arrived in Nairobi with our hair long and stiff like beach grass, and our bush shorts torn and still covered with burrs. Sights like us were common, and even when we sat at the Thorn Tree Bar at the New Stanley, rummaging through our mail, we elicited few stares. For one week we did all the things which suddenly seemed to be essential to our lives: we ordered only the very best wines, ate only French food, groomed our appearances and enjoyed wearing coats and ties and dresses. The surge of people and the babble of talk intoxicated us. We rushed not out of necessity but because we considered any slower rate inexcusable.

The most convenient meeting place was the Long Bar of the New Stanley, where the drinking began long before midday and lasted until that moment when it seemed wise to move to more comfortable surroundings. It is, as its name implies, a bar efficiently designed so that a lot of people can get a lot of drinks all at the same time. Everything from the flooring to the walls is indestructible. Here is where the old-timers, grumbling about one another, convene before lunch to encounter people they thought had died long ago, where game wardens and khaki-clad farmers carrying worn briefcases have "one last drink" before they head off into "the blue," and where clients toast their hunters while waiting for their equipment to be packed onto the trucks. For many it is the one place in Nairobi which is guaranteed never to change: the bartenders always give menacing glances to those who don't tip, an old crippled beggar ("the richest man in Nairobi") has not missed a day in recorded history, and the general tone of backslapping banter, after many years, remains as

Now, reader, I am about to take you up to Nairobi. First I will let you into a secret which may repay you for the money you have squandered in buying this book . . . Take a few bottles of soda and a little whiskey; even if you do not need them yourself you will find yourself popular with fellow travelers who have not been equally provident. Failing this, take a corkscrew, as someone is sure to have a bottle and no corkscrew; lending yours will establish a claim on his hospitality.

— *Captain C. H. Stigand,*
The Land of Zinj, 1913

it was. Although there are no annual dues, no list of members or assessments, the Long Bar is, in the purest sense of the word, a club. Temporary memberships have traditionally been made available to anybody who is willing to buy the drinks.

"Hoppy" Marshall generally chose a seat next to his caricature hanging on the wall. He was considered a bastion of the Long Bar and a certain attraction for all newcomers. His nickname derived from a youthful disability of the knee which forced him, even when seated, to keep one of his legs perfectly stiff. "Right now my life's at a low point — an absolute washout," he said to me. "I'm a debt collector for the bloody electric company. But you can be sure I've had some fun in my day." It all began, he explained, when he rose from the ranks of the street urchins in London's Soho to become the owner of the first two-penny "gaff" (movie house) under a railway arch. ("Tuppence for the world's greatest miracle.") It was a great success, although the projector ceased to operate whenever trains ran overhead. His first disaster struck when he found himself stranded in East Africa a few years later with several hundred thousand feet of film which, contrary to what he had expected, was not in great demand even at a farthing a foot. "Hoppy" almost immediately went to work as a doctor in Nairobi because, as he explained, even without a degree he had "a flair for surgery." A succession of careers followed, leading to the accumulation and almost immediate disposal of several fortunes. Finally, as a middle-aged man he settled down to being Nairobi's hangman. His fees were unabashedly discriminatory. "I used to hang Africans for five shillings [70 cents], Europeans for two hundred shillings [$28], and Indians for nothing." When business slowed down he opened a bar outside of Nairobi but was forced to close down several years later during the Mau Mau emergency. "I love Kenya," he told me, "because here I've been able to do so many things that people thought couldn't be done." Again he said, "Right now, however, it's a bit of a washout," and then tossing back the last of his beer he hurried to his job as debt collector.

Another occasional visitor to the Long Bar was H. K. Binks, the oldest living inhabitant of Nairobi. I met him at his house near the Ngong Road and he fixed me with his hunter's eyes, now watery and faded, as though he were sizing me up for a heart shot. Ever since 1900, when he had arrived in East Africa with eighteen pounds in his pocket, through his years as a pioneer farmer in Kikuyu country, then as photographer of Paul Rainey's, Fritz Schindelar's and Philip Percival's safaris, and finally as a hunter himself, he has treated events and people with an objective mind. "After all," he said, "I am a chemist by profession." (Later he was to explain: "If I hadn't left my little Yorkshire village I'd still be selling castor oil.") Binks did not regret the passing of the old days. He talked briefly about the foot safaris, the blisters, the thirst, the great trophies and the smell of a campfire from far away. He stopped to listen to the cars racing past his house en route to the suburbs and said, "We used to have as many as one hundred and twenty porters adjusting their loads in front of the Norfolk Hotel. I must say the old pageantry was wonderful and effective, but," and here he paused momentarily, "personally I prefer the motor car."

The spirit of a glad age full of convictions lingered wherever I went. I caught it at the Muthaiga Club, at the sight of tidy farms on the feet of the Ngong Hills, in the faces of forgotten servants at the Norfolk Hotel; and when I left Nairobi I felt it once again on the verandas of Thompson's Falls and Nanyuki — old men self-consciously looking for new hopes or else defeatedly cherishing old ambitions. In the bush the memories were not maudlin. In the cold mornings in camp as we drank hot coffee we watched the faces of the small *totos* and the old

Two old ladies discussing a recent scandal at the Muthaiga Club in Nairobi: "Shocking! But, mind you, I've heard worse."

mzees as they exclaimed over what were for them new adventures of the mind. Thoughts passed between them through exclamations and sighs. Sometimes in the desert country I caught a feeling of permanence in the sharp, clear faces of those who walked from the edge of the distance to lean on their sticks and pay us their salaams. I thought I also found it in the old familiarity between strangers passing each other on roads, sharing the shadows of dust clouds and the language of maps.

But memories belong to only a shadow life. Today there is an urgency which begins in Nairobi and spreads through Kenya like an electrical storm. In every part of the country, it seems, people are learning how to rush and to shout, impatient with a former way of life. Progress is the trademark of all that is unknown and foreign. The lip-thundering enthusiasm for change has caught hold of Africa's imagination, and a new day characterized by an indiscriminate mixture of good and bad is dawning. There is a hope among the new leaders of Africa that any solution, provided it does not savor of the words "colonialism" and "imperialism," will erase the misery of deprived people. And although men do not grow less hungry by possessing dignity in their racial distinctiveness and by handing down their own judgments, they at least have less time to worry about the emptiness in their stomachs.

Today the spirit of the pioneer has been leached from the land. An era of self-certainty is being replaced by one of doubt and compromise. Time which was once thought to stand still is demonstrating to the last survivors of a bold generation that it indeed waits for no man. Today in Africa there is a new white man, but he is merely a bird of

passage, flying in from cold, damp places to fulfill the
terms of a contract. Unlike the first settlers he is burdened
with a need for security and comfort at the expense of his
sense of adventure. His roots do not penetrate the land, as
did those of the pioneers, but spread through the over-
crowded world of specialization where men are judged in
terms of university degrees and years of experience. The
new Africa is an unfriendly place for those who prided
themselves on their ability to learn from nature since it, the
last of the wild places, has acquired the common touch.

Tony Dyer, president of the East African Professional
Hunters' Association, could see the pockmarked desert of
the Northern Frontier District from his farm. I had been
waiting for him on the stoep of his home all afternoon, and
when the gray dusk light began to disguise the shape of
the horizon I heard the sound of his plane and soon I saw it
floating like a shadow from the clouds onto a grass field
behind a hill. After the noise of the engine had ceased,
Dyer, dressed in bush clothes and carrying a briefcase, approached me. He had a lean runner's body which coiled
and uncoiled as though it were used to long walks. Inside
the house he poured himself a Scotch and sat down in a
chair. After a while he explained that he had given up hunting and now was merely the official spokesman for the other
hunters. He was young enough to have caught only a fleeting glimpse of Kenya as an unspoiled land, and today he
was able to indulge those memories by living away from
the hustle of cities and crowds. "When I began hunting,"
he explained, "I was the baby of the group. I learned from
the old-timers that the only way to travel to the hunting

grounds was without the use of roads." When he began his career, a drive from Nairobi overland to Lake Victoria along game trails was considered an inconsequential trip. There were no four-wheel drive vehicles then, only Ford trucks. Even as late as the Second World War most rivers were crossed at natural fords, since there were few bridges in East Africa. If fords were nonexistent the safari came to a halt and everyone set to work to construct a temporary bridge or a drift. If the trucks broke down they were repaired on the spot with whatever materials were available: bearings out of pigskin, brake linings out of cowhide, and broken spokes strengthened with green rawhide. Dyer's first one hundred thousand miles of safari driving were done in this manner. "It was a life," he said, "which separated the idle from the active. Even the clients had to struggle." In the early days of the Colony, safari clients were generally dedicated hunters who had spent most of their lives stalking wild animals. One of Dyer's clients was a man who had shot Marco Polo sheep in China the year Dyer was born. Safaris rarely lasted for less than four months, with several weeks on either end for the long boat trip out and back from Africa. "What changed the safari," Dyer explained, "was the Land Rover. Today with a four-wheel drive vehicle you can move about in reasonable comfort. Sand and mud became negotiable without the driver ever having to get out of the cab. In addition to the dedicated sportsmen, a new type of client has begun to hunt. Today the whole business is status-oriented. What's more important than the hunt, it seems, is talking about the hunt. The professional hunter's concern today is not necessarily providing clients with trophies but making sure they

I count the days of my trip in malaria pills.
— *American tourist in Africa*

are comfortable and well entertained. He's merely a
caterer." Only a handful of the old clients are returning to
Kenya, according to Dyer, because the hunting they used
to do is not possible today. There is an American, for instance, who has been coming out regularly since the late
thirties. He has collected record trophies of almost every
species of animal, and now when he goes on safari he
rarely leaves camp. His friends do all the hunting and
when they return in the evening he may recount his adventures.

For Dyer the end of the hunt was not necessarily the end
of a way of life. There were still numberless ways of re-cre-
ating the spirit of the frontier: millions of square miles of
bush still to be cut into ranches and vast landscapes yet to
be seen. Dyer was anxious to be among the last of the bush
specialists, but he sensed that his life was at best synthetic
in the new Africa. For him the hunt had assumed an abstract form: he no longer required a high-powered rifle
since he had lived for the anticipatory pleasure of the
stalk, the badinage of animal temperaments, the endless
discussions with the trackers, and the thrill of piecing together the faint clues to what may be a great trophy. The
tragedy was that the manly natures which upheld this patient sport were being corrupted. So, like a sea captain who
had retired from his ship to the beach, Dyer had ceased
being a hunter. He was content that from his ranch he
could view the great desert which stretched to the borders
of Somalia and Ethiopia. It was, he said, like being on the
edge of the great beyond.

Unlike Dyer, George Adamson, another member of the
bush fraternity, had a poor view. His camp, made of reeds

and *makuti* poles and surrounded by a high wire fence, was locked in by scrubby bush and a row of rocky hills. When I arrived, a lion, limping from a recent fight with one of its rivals, bounded from the deep grass and rubbed its neck against our legs. George Adamson introduced it to us as Ugas, and all of us watched as it tried to dislodge the rigid body of a recently shot zebra from the back of a truck. Finally, after we had helped by heaving the carcass over the side, Ugas ripped open the stomach and chewed on its intestines. The other lions that lived with George Adamson appeared from the bush and joined in the orgy of meat. The zebra was dragged a hundred yards from the camp, but still we heard the crunching of its bones, and in the late afternoon the wind switched and the fetid smell of decay blew at us in the camp. We took off our shirts because of the muggy heat, smoked cigars and drank tea in an effort to forget the animal smell. Late at night when the others had gone to bed, George Adamson and I opened the gates and walked out among the lions. A female was lapping water from a trough near the fence. She nuzzled up against us, pressing her face into our palms, her shoulders against our hips and then crept, almost unnoticed, through the half-opened gates into the camp. "A clever trick," George mumbled to himself, and then we followed her into the little reed shelter where she was trying to climb onto the table. George tugged at her neck and when this appeared hopeless he slowly coaxed her out with soft Somali words. Much later, after the moon had risen, I lay on my camp bed and saw the lions jump onto the roof of what served as a garage, and throughout the night I heard the rumblings of their stomachs and the heavy sound of splashing as they urinated onto the hood of the Land Rover.

Terence Adamson was staying with his brother George. They both were strong-muscled men, with bodies scarred by their encounters with wild animals. Whenever they spoke their eyes cast about over the dry, thorny ground looking for something familiar to set upon. Throughout their lives they had been used to dealing with things over which they had an advantage; equality made them uneasy and, sometimes, embarrassed. They avoided "hellos" and "good-byes" and other formalities, for they conceived of themselves merely as observers of nature and sublimated their human natures to their surroundings.

Very rarely did George speak of himself. Once he mentioned unassumingly that his wife had written a book about their pet lioness. In the film that was subsequently made of it, he explained, a total of twenty-two lions was used. He had kept several of them and he was studying them as they readapted themselves to the wilds. A wild animal, George maintained, was rarely dangerous until put behind bars. He had found making the film interesting but he had declined the film company's invitation to see the premiere. "Too many people inside the cinema," he explained.

In a bar, after I had left George Adamson's camp, an old man squinted his eyes and, leaning back into a wicker chair, said, "There are a lot of stories about George Adamson which will never be known. Did you ever hear, for instance, that he made the first recorded crossing of Lake Rudolf?" It had happened out of necessity, the old man explained. In 1934 Adamson and a friend were prospecting for gold on the eastern shores of the lake. After six months with no success they ran out of food and decided to cross the lake by boat rather than walk two hundred miles to the nearest Indian *duka*. They constructed a small boat out of acacia branches which they tied together with leather thongs. During the night before their planned departure jackals ate the thongs and the boat collapsed. Their energy waning because of the lack of food, the two men rebuilt the boat using bits of bark. When they were about to set sail a storm broke and once again they were delayed. Finally, as though propelled merely by instinct for they had not eaten for almost a week, they began to row across the thirty-mile-wide lake. After four hours they gave up all hope when they heard a noise like a storm, but they soon discovered that it was the croaking of frogs. After rowing for a total of six hours, their hands bleeding, they reached the western shores of the lake just in time to watch a storm break. They walked for three days, and at the limits of their energy they came upon a Turkana village where they were fed and cared for.

The African bartender had heard the old man telling me the story and he too had known George Adamson. "My people," he said, "call him *mzee*, the old man. He is a wise old man because he knew that his lions would make him rich. Why else would he have tamed them?"

From Meru to the coast I thought of what Joy Adamson, George's wife, had said to me. Over a cold lunch of Spam in the shade of a fig tree near her camp she had sought to

explain to me why she lived in the bush. Finally she began to tell me about Elsa, her pet lioness, "There was no reason why we should have loved each other: I a human being, and both of us females. It was a love between two worlds, a love which took me back to the roots of my existence. I believe all this had a message for human beings, bringing them, as it brought me, back to reality. I don't know what it was — certainly it was more than just a symbol for it seemed to mean something to everybody."

Pippa, a wild cheetah whom she had befriended since Elsa's death, had been missing for several weeks. Hours before we arrived at her camp it had returned, acknowledging an old friendship by silently rubbing itself against her legs. Hidden in the grass behind it were its kittens, and one by one it picked them up in its mouth and brought them for her to examine. "I wish I could tell you why this animal is to me more than just a pet," she continued. "Most of us, I think, are living a detached existence, an artificial one, lost in our own creations and unaware of the basic creation of life. I think it's all because man is over-specialized and has lost the general truths about life. To me it seems that he has put too much into his brain, making all the superficialities of life far more important than they deserve to be. There is no room left in this world for the man with the general outlook. Unless he escapes to the timeless places as I have done, he cannot appreciate life in its pure, broad and simple reality."

All of a sudden, as I drove along the corrugated road to the coast, I saw Africa as I had once seen the floor of the Rift from an airplane: the tilled fields, the vacuous expanse of Lake Hannington, the thin metallic sheen of the untouched lands half in the sunlight, half in the shade, all waiting to breathe. The emptiness was being filled with man's objects and ever so slowly the world was being given a purpose. It seemed to me that where once there had been only a future without an end now there was a goal and hence a deadline. Africa was picking up its many legs, like some mythological monster, and was clumsily making its way to the edge of the cliff.

It seemed to me during that moment as I sped along the narrow road toward the coast that there had been too much history in Africa, too many lifetimes squeezed into a handful of years, too many convictions destroyed by accidents and aberrations. Those who came to change the old order refused to believe that a new order might ever replace theirs. Africa is once again black Africa, and in a tradition common to all races when they have lost faith in themselves, goals are achieved by bloodlettings. The white man and the black man have lost faith in ideals and today throats are slit for the merest trifles. Just as the great explorer Karl Peters once shot his cook-boy for underdoing the potatoes, today the "mission boys" watch the nuns burn to death because of the color of their skins. Blood has mixed with other blood, and deaths, however warranted, are ultimately equal to those which were in vain. Black is made white, bad is made good, the past is hidden in the hopes of the future with the slash of the ubiquitous *panga*.

Not until I had reached the coast of Kenya did I realize how effective those knives had been, how truly dead, in one sense, the era of the white man was. A rule of brash paternalism had fallen, and within the ranks of those who accepted its end as their defeat, self-doubt, bitterness and escapism had followed. I began to believe that their pioneering spirit had only been part of a human phase, and the generalities of life that they had once asserted had now yielded to personal grievances.

In Lamu, an island off the coast of Kenya, the heavy, rust-producing climate leaves little hope for a new life. For three thousand years foreigners have used the island as the last outpost of their command: first the Assyrians, then the Persians under the legendary Harun al-Rashid, later the Portuguese and finally the British. Wars were common, and today on a beach near the harbor the bones of conquerors and conquered can still be seen half-buried in the sand. At the sight of a bag of sequins deadly enemies were known to throw down their arms and forget their differences, while smothering each other with flattery and dynastic matchmaking. Until the beginning of the twentieth century no Arabic lady worthy of her rank would dare walk the streets without at least four slaves to hold a silk canopy over her head. In January of every year high-pooped dhows sailed like swallows into the muddy port, bringing with them cargoes from the caliphates and sheikhdoms along the Persian Gulf. When they set sail on the prevailing winds they took with them ambergris, bêche-de-mer, a delicacy which seasonally floats onto the beaches of East Africa, and mangrove poles, which were used as beams throughout the Arabian Peninsula. Prostitutes, their feet and the palms of their hands painted with henna, and their eyelids covered with kohl, lined the harbor front, their smell of jasmine invading the rank odor of the beach.

Since 1872 when the British-India Mail Steamship Company began to put into Lamu once a month, the island has acquired a reputation as a haven for remittance men and derelicts. In 1895 the island was invaded by a communistic group called the Freelanders who believed in both joint ownership of land and communal rights to the women. The group was composed of Austrians, Britishers, Danes and Germans, variously described as swindlers, drunkards, agitators, thieves and lunatics. Their plan was to proceed along the Tana River into the interior of Africa and found a colony near Mount Kenya, but because of violent quarrels, a shortage of capital, and bad planning they never left Lamu. After several months, their last resources exhausted, they went their own ways. Other Europeans, some more respectable, have followed them. Rider Haggard's brother, "Juba" Joe, Percy Petley, Jerry Pink, and Henri Burnier, the Swiss Nestlé heir, are all remembered by the older inhabitants of the island. "Coconut" Charlie, another legend, was in charge of a shipping office for more than twenty years. Every day, wearing a stiff collar and a white suit, and carrying a briefcase, he punctually paraded along the waterfront to his office. Even toward the end of his life when Lamu was no longer visited by the mailships he maintained strict office hours, and regularly on Wednesdays he still locked himself in his hot office with a sign over the door reading "Do not disturb. Mail day," while he memorized old train schedules from the British Railways.

Today the high-pooped dhows no longer cross the Indian Ocean to Lamu; mangrove poles, slaves and cloves are not marketable, and the chief concern, as elsewhere in Africa, is to live from day to day. The streets, wide enough to allow two donkeys to pass, are bordered by sewage troughs. The windows of all the houses are shuttered, but sometimes, through half-opened doors, one can catch the

smell of burning incense and hear the sleepless songs of
Arabia. A police boat, used in former times to patrol the
coast, rides ineffectively at anchor.

"Darky" Bryanton, a Cockney who wears Arab clothes,
runs Petley's Inn, the only hotel in Lamu. A teak and brass
door, facing onto the harbor, leads into the bar, where in
the flickering shadows of kerosene lamps Sikhs, Arabs and
a few Europeans struggle to cure the unquenchable thirst
of the coast. The dining room, on a balcony above the bar,
is accessible by means of a narrow, unlit staircase and a
long corridor smelling of mildew. From here the view is of
coastal dhows lying on their sides in the mud and of a row
of rusted cannons bordering the sea front. In the evening
the sound of the lamplighter making his rounds mixes
with the sounds of Oriental music.

"Abdulla and Allen, Merchants: Tea, Trinkets, Finery
& General Curious Articles. Houses Too Late," reads a
sign over a door in a side street. At the top of a long wind-
ing staircase, in a room decorated with bucolic scenes of
England, lay "Baa" Allen, suffering from malaria. He
raised himself on an elbow to greet me and then fell back
onto the bed. He would be better tomorrow, he explained.
"The bloody disease strikes me periodically." His face was
sallow and pasty, his hands sticky as though they had been
clenched for some time. Sweat was bubbling over his tem-
ples and he was trembling slightly. "I want to get away,"
he whispered to me. "I last saw England in nineteen
twenty-six, and now I want to return." Through half-
shuttered windows I could see the rows of corrugated iron
roofs, hung up like washing, and the pied crows settling on them with echoing crashes. In the harbor bare-
chested Arabs were filing barnacles off the bottoms of their

dhows. "You see," he continued, "I don't like these Bantu people who control Africa. I don't like their everlasting mediocrity. My people are the Somalis and the desert nomads. Nothing petty about them: they'd rather have a thousand cattle, not just thirty. They have a clean, sweet smell about them, of milk and the musky odor of their camels' dung. If only you knew what the cleanliness of open places is like or what joy there is in getting sweet water from the wells there. But I realize there is no longer any life for me up there and so it's time for me to be going home." A little brown-skinned girl who had been left in his care was playing on the veranda and her girlish laughter filtered into the room. "Little devil that Somali girl is," he said half to himself. He squinted his eyes to peer out through the slats of the door into the sunlight, but all he could see was the glare. He closed his eyes and cursed his malaria.

"*Bwana* Kikapu," another European, lived by himself in an Arab house on the far side of Lamu. When I arrived he was sitting on his veranda fanning himself. After having lived for so many years in Africa, he said to me, he should have been used to the heat. The old man went inside the house and brought out two journals which he said had belonged to his father who had been a captain of a whaling ship. The last entry had been made in 1908, inscribed after a year's trip to the Arctic during which only one whale had been boated. "He never went on board a ship again," the old man said. "When I went off to Africa a few years later Dad said to me 'I don't suppose I'll ever see you again,' and he was right: I've never gone home. Right now I'm feeling a bit like he did when he returned to Scotland in 1908. It's as though I too have boated my last whale. It's been a good life here in Africa but in a few years it's not going to be worth living. Right now I'm waiting to get away to Australia. I'll sail on the first boat that has a berth for me." Lamu, he explained to me, had been ideal for him because it was so inexpensive. The rent on his house was six dollars a month and his total monthly expenses came to forty-three dollars. "It's a good place to be poor in," he continued. "It never changes — sort of a half-dead, half-alive place. White people generally come here because they can't get along with other whites." The old man had finished the last of his detective novels, and since the mails were unpredictable there was little chance he would get a new shipment for several months. "The first boat that has a bunk for me and I'll be off to Australia," he murmured once again as I left.

"Funny," Darky Bryanton later told me. "He's been saying that for the past four years."

Several nights later we sat with a group of bare-chested men around a bar in Malindi. A kerosene lamp hanging from the thatched roof was making the shadows of our drinks waver and stretch along the table, while nearby the sea was lapping against the coral shelf of the beach. At first the men around the table had talked in parables to avoid personal complicity in their stories, but as the night progressed defenses vanished. The Englishman wearing a diminutive bathing suit laughed about being cashiered from the Welsh Guards, and later swore at the mention of his last wife, an Afro-Arab stripper, who three weeks previously had stabbed him with a knive. To his right, a Dane described how he had been shot by the wife of a famous lord when he was manager of her Rift Valley farm. "You see," he explained, "she realized that I knew a lot about her

Today Africa has gone away. Europeans in this country no longer care or worry because it is no longer theirs.
— Told to me by Pat Hemingway

that I shouldn't have known. I did something silly one night: I said to her, 'Since I know too much, you have only one alternative and that is to shoot me. You'll find a revolver in the top drawer of my bureau.' The next I remember was waking up in the hospital with a hole in my shoulder. My assassin was so terribly embarrassed by the whole matter that she went down to the coast for a holiday."

A new round of drinks arrived on the table and once more there was a rush of conversation. We talked of the Happy Valley, of prewar notoriety, where men played bridge for each others' wives, where "visiting rights" to the women were established by hat pools and where, in its latter days, rifle shots were regularly exchanged between neighbors. "Kenya," someone at the table joked, "is a land where men are men and women wide open spaces." We spoke of the "Khaki Highlands," so called because most of the children of the Europeans were off-white, and of the lonely rancher in Rumuruti who invited the only other European in the area to a black-tie dinner party and over the candle-lit table carried on imaginary conversations with duchesses and lord-mayors. It was late, and soon each of us fell silent and listened to the waves rustling across the coral shelf and the winds whispering through the high fronds of the palms.

The last I saw of the coast was the rush of greenery through the porthole of the Dakota and a glimpse of the Giriama people on the edge of the runway. The burst of power from the engines forced us into the backs of our seats and with our arms we braced ourselves against the bouncing of the wheels across the rutted grass strip. The hot, luxuriant air of the coast vanished and was replaced by the smell of metal and leather. Fleetingly I saw Malindi's unprotected harbor, where fishing boats wrestled with their anchor lines. The coffee-colored beach and the windswept expanse of Formosa Bay unfolded to the north, but within seconds the silver wing of the plane obscured it as we began to climb up over the African continent.

It was evening and the more we climbed into the west the brighter the sky grew. Our course to Nairobi was slightly north of the route of the early explorers, but soon, as we climbed, we began to see their country: the Taru Desert below us and to the south the Taita Hills, lying like half-eaten fruit. Ahead of us lay the high country of Kenya, the end of their long safari. I sensed that the view from the porthole added something to the view I once had had of Ol Bolossat and Lake Hannington, and perhaps, I thought, as I looked at the miles of untouched land, the old Africa had not really come to a close.

While the plane climbed into the thin air, I thought of the new breed of pioneers I had met in Kenya; I thought of Ritchie Barbour, a rough, smiling Yorkshireman, who had sold his farm in England at the height of the Mau Mau emergency, bought an old car and driven his family across the Sahara to their new farm in Kenya. "In England," he explained, "the majority of farmers were keeping ahead and making a profit. Here in Africa it was different, for most farmers were behind and needed help. That's why it's been so much fun. Today my sons and I control the largest complex of intensive mixed farming in Kenya. In addition to that I would venture to say that our herd of Ayreshires is the best in Africa." He put his hand into a bucket of wheat and let the grains run between his crusty fingers. "What's made us do so well," he continued, "is our policy of qualified gambling. Almost every chance we've taken has paid off."

*Were I offered my life
again I expect I would
make the same mis-
takes, I know I would
want to plant and tend,
to build houses and
make dams, to answer
the challenge of a new
horizon, and wonder at
man and Nature's
eternal unity and
blessed variation.*

— *Gerard Wallop,
Earl of
Portsmouth,*
A Knot of Roots

At the foot of Mount Elgon I spoke to the Earl of Portsmouth, also a recent arrival. I met him among his herd of Brown Swiss cattle, which were lumbering down from the upland pastures. He led me into the quiet seclusion of his garden where he knelt down and stroked one of his dogs. His face, full of the shadows of thought and sensitivity, was leathery from a life in the out-of-doors. He explained to me that as a boy he had lived in the horse and cattle country of northern Wyoming. Later, once he had finished Oxford, he took over the management of Farleigh Wallop, his family estate in Hampshire, and after several years, he succeeded in making it self-supporting. He was elected to the House of Commons and later, having become the Earl of Portsmouth, served in the House of Lords. Late in life, having decided that there was little left for him to do in England, he settled in Africa. In England, he felt, the people with talent were being pushed aside in favor of the common good, but in Africa there would be need of his talents. The headlong progress of the age seemed to be reducing man's sense of values to double-entry bookkeeping. After leaving England he wrote about his life there in *A Knot of Roots*. "The more we received a modern education the more spiritually illiterate we were becoming. The more we watched, be it sport, cinema, and later television, the less we did. The more we heard the less we listened, the more we ate of preserved and processed foods the less we truly digested. The more we learned of how our psyches worked the less sound our minds became."

All around us in the garden the night noises had set in. Portsmouth was smoking a cigarette and staring into the reaches of the darkness spread over the valley below us. "In my heart," he had once written, "is the true aristocratic claim to be putting more into African life than I take from it. If I can help the economy well and good; if however humbly I can help the long safari of the mind across a thousand years of bitter experience in a generation, well and better." He must have been smiling, for after a brief pause he flicked his cigarette away and said to me, "What I am so proud about in my short stay here in Africa is that the Africans I employ have begun to trust me. They come to me, '*Bwana* Lordee' as I am called, and pour their hearts out. You cannot believe the agonies the twentieth century has made them suffer. I think I often can help them, not because I understand them necessarily but because my presence is cathartic to them. I tell them that there is only one thing that gives comfort and that is human love. And in a very small way," and here he paused, "but certainly in the highest sense, they can get their love from me."

By now it was dark. Through the portholes of the plane I saw the red glow from the exhaust of the engine and beyond it the faint shadows of cumulus clouds bobbing in the high thin air. The woman sitting next to me lit a cigarette. When I had first taken my seat I had noticed her, like a fading figurehead from the prow of a tall ship. Her hands, covered with calluses, resembled old taproots, and her sunburned face seemed to be lost in a sea of white hair.

She was a pioneer of Kenya, she explained to me. She leaned back into the seat and puffed on her cigarette. With her parents, she continued, she had trekked onto the highlands in an ox wagon. She remembered the thatched hut which was their first home in Kenya, the struggle the family had made to discover what crops grew best, the mornings when they found that elephants had trampled the *shamba* and the nights when lions slept on the veranda.

She paused for a second to look out into the night through the porthole. She lit another cigarette and told me about her old servants, of those who had broken the trust to take the Mau Mau oath and of the others who even to this day remain loyal.

The plane began to lose altitude and out of the starboard window I saw the lights of Machakos and Athi. Somewhere to the right of the wing tip was her old farm. "It was sold last week," she explained. "I'd always been able to run it by myself ever since my parents died, but these days everything has begun to change. This country no longer belongs to white people like you and me." She paused to look out the window. "I'm not bitter that the black man has finally come into his own but I know that there is no place left for me out here." The airplane was making its final approach and soon I saw the lights of the runway flashing under the wings and felt a soft nudge as the tires met the runway. "Tomorrow I'm booked on a flight to Australia. I've already bought a farm out there and I plan to start all over again."

CHAPTER VI

*Up till his death the country had been the Happy Hunting
Grounds, now it was slowly changing and turning into a
business proposition. Some standards were lowered when
he went: a standard of wit, as it was soon felt, — and
such a thing is sad in a colony; a standard of gallantry,
— soon after his death people began to talk of their troubles; a standard of humanity.*

— Isak Dinesen, *Out of Africa*

For two days we had not seen water; every river we crossed was dry and the plateau to the west which was the hope of all the surrounding country looked burned and desiccated like the desert. Since leaving the settlement of Lodwar we had been driving south across the flinty land praying that the Land Rover's springs would last and hoping that soon we would be able to fill our jerricans with water. On several occasions when we saw vultures circling in the distance we tried to guess what mummified carcass had attracted their attention. A Turkana warrior, tall and straight like an ancient Egyptian, once rode with us on the hood of the car. After several miles he waved his spear for us to stop and then vanished into the shimmer of the thermals to meet his flock of goats. Even in the late afternoon the sun made few shadows and the air, blowing through the ventilators, was no comfort.

I heard the sound of rushing water just as we came in sight of a mission station, a flat modern building which, in the light of the moon, looked as though it could only have bubbled up from the center of the earth. From a row of huts clinging to the compound like tick birds came the smell of wood smoke and the soft murmuring of voices. For a second we sat in the car adjusting our eyes to the stillness and then, stepping across the loose rock, we followed the sound of the rushing water to the edge of a small cliff.

Below us a waterfall tumbled from a hot spring into a shallow pool. The water, bright with moonlight, might have contained a thousand fish darting with the speed of light from one side to the other. Here was the king of all water holes: we had left the dry land.

We dove naked into the pool and then swam into the turmoil of the heated water under the falls. We lay on our backs and let ourselves be nudged by the current across the gravel to where the water was cool. We felt nothing except the occasional scraping of the gravel against the backs of our legs and the long stroking fingers of the current through our hair. Hours might have passed as we lay motionless watching the night sky.

Before the moon had set I heard a metallic sound from the cliff, and, looking up, I saw two Pokot warriors stepping over the boulders to the pool where we lay. At the edge of the water they lifted the folds of their skirts and, without hesitation, crossed in single file to the other side. Their hair, intricately plaited and covered with mud, was lacquered by the moonlight and their spears and the coiled copper around their arms glistened with a desert polish. It seemed to us, lying in the shadows holding our breaths, that just as they scorned the water they might also not need to eat food, sleep or breathe air. For them water was where the strong succumb and the weak fail, where only the outsiders find peace, where the cattle and goats must eventually be led and where hope is restored only temporarily.

In the morning we left. We drove once again into the dust and the flinty basalt, into the one color and the one life of the desert. But soon we noticed that the country began to change: tortured hills, which from the air might have looked like waves on an oily sea, locked us in and a film of olive-gray vegetation began to grow between the rocks. As soon as we passed Lake Baringo, which looked like a trench filled with hemlock, the road began to climb into the higher country. Our landmarks now were no longer the junctions of car tracks, but were corrugated iron settlements of naked children and sewing machines and Indian merchants. The road improved and we drove faster.

At Nakuru we joined the main tarmac road. It was Sunday and on the veranda of the hotel men were dressed in suits and ties. In the center of each of the wide avenues of the town were islands of mown grass and trimmed bougainvillea. We did not stop and soon we were on the road to Nairobi. It stretched ahead of us in a straight line until it reached the foot of the Rift, and then, snakelike, it crawled into the highlands. Ahead of us, to the south, we were able to see limitlessly along the floor of the Rift and in the rippled distance, like phantoms, I saw rain clouds. They were scurrying along the flat lands followed by gray shadows. The volcano of Suswa, once clearly visible, now vanished. The gloom converged on us with a monstrous sense of mission as we hurried to reach the foot of the escarpment and begin the climb into the green Kikuyu country.

As soon as we began the ascent of the Rift wall thunder exploded over our heads and, within seconds, the rains were upon us. At first big drops fell onto the car, steaming where it was hot, but soon they fell in earnest, beating on the roof like gunfire and dripping through the invisible cracks in the welding. The distances were lost from sight and the road, like a ribbon being coiled, disappeared in the rain above our heads.

Briefly, as the car inched along the tortuous road, I remembered my climb up Kilimanjaro. The sound of our Chagga porters' barefoot treading along the mountain trail seemed to filter into the cab of the Land Rover, and once more I was breathing the short acid breaths of the high altitudes. I remembered my hope in the last hut at 15,520 feet, as we had waited for the guide to tell us to ready ourselves for the final test, that the view from the top would be the ultimate in the whole of Africa. All through the black climb along the scree, the falling and cursing and nausea, the wait and the stillness looking through the oyster mouth of a cave halfway there, I had believed in victory. I thought I sensed what John Rebman must have felt when in 1845 he was the first white man to see the silver dome of Kilimanjaro, or what stirred the blood of Hans Meyer when in 1889 he stood on the crater, the highest man in Africa. A breath and then a feeling of desperation with the next step over the scree: the torture of struggling forward and slipping back.

We had reached the top at dawn. I fell onto the rock and looked through shuttered eyes at the blue-green stillness of the glacier. Nature was in its most elemental form. Around us were only rocks and ice and empty, almost airless, space. We were above the eagles and the clouds in a place where not even the spirits would live. But men had been here: they had come and gone, like me, in short hopes of glory, leaving their initials and signs and tatters as proof that even the highest had been deflowered.

We had returned to the hut with giant steps and soon

I don't know what my father saw in Kilimanjaro. It looks great from a distance but it lets you down when you get close to it.

— Told to me by Pat Hemingway

after we began the return trek across the saddle and then into the "red-hot poker" country. I had looked over my shoulder and seen once again the rounded peak of Kilimanjaro. It looked like an anthill that had been built and destroyed by many generations of little bodies. I thought of the leopard that had reached the edge of the glacier and died there, and the buffalo which had been found on a precipice at sixteen thousand feet.

The rain was now beating even more fiercely on the roof of the car as we climbed the wall of the Rift. The windshield wipers moved too slowly to clean the rivers that sluiced across the glass. Many months of dust were being washed from the body of the Land Rover and for once it looked respectable.

It had rained as heavily on Mount M'Gahinga in Uganda several years before, when we had been looking for the mountain gorilla; all day as we climbed through the bamboo and moss the rain dripped on us through the heavy overgrowth. At night we camped high up among the wild celery and in the early morning our porters came shouting into camp to tell us that gorillas were nearby. We set out and in a short distance we saw the animals on the far side of a *donga*, their bullet heads framed in the trees by the vegetation. We crept on all fours through the dripping nettle. Far down in the valley a hoopoe whistled. Suddenly a gorilla rose in front of us, bellowing. It stared at us with a bearing altogether too familiar, as of a huge, fine man of a different race. Briefly it was ferocious, then indignant, and finally scared. With one last bellow it lowered itself onto all fours and moved noisily through the bush, leaving us shaken by its presence.

Two years later I returned to see the gorilla but it was

gone from the mountain. We ventured along the elephant trails, through the mud and the dripping ferns, pretending as a last measure to feel the presence of another life near us. We searched and finally when it was late retraced our steps down the mountain in the dark. Reuben, our guide, shook his head and repeated once again that the gorillas had gone for good. "Hunters," he murmured innocently.

The thunder was now far to the north, and below us the haze which had covered the floor of the Rift like a blanket was thinning. I thought of my last meeting with Binks, the oldest living resident of Nairobi, still happy with the home he had built for himself in 1910. The day before I arrived, he had been beaten up and robbed. His wife told me how the two thieves had crept through the windows of the house and hit "Pop" over his head while he was asleep. "They came to the wrong place," the old man later said, rubbing the bandages over his eye. "The only valuable things they could find were a few bottles of drink and a frayed tablecloth." He stared out through the trees which separated his house from the ever-expanding town of Nairobi. "This is the fourth time I've been robbed in the past three years," he told me. "The average person would be annoyed but not I. It's the same as what happened many years ago when five hundred people got on a ship in England and appropriated that plot of land called America. The white man has not set a very good example, has he?" Far beyond the evening traffic were the Ngong Hills. We both looked there as they were the farthest objects to be seen from Binks's house. The old man raised his arm and tried to point out to me the grave of a famous hunter high in the hills. He was about to tell me a story but something,

perhaps the noise of the passing cars, interrupted him, and
he fell silent.

There had been a racing-car meet at Nakuru that afternoon and, before we reached the top of the Rift, I saw in
my rearview mirror a stream of fast cars approaching.
Soon they were passing us, their engines revving as they
accelerated. By the time we reached the top of the Rift we
were behind them. Once again we were alone. The rain
clouds were now to the north and the bowl of the Rift was
cast in sunlight. The rain had stopped and I opened the
window. The air was new and full of the smells of young
shoots and rich loam. We could have been anywhere.